Hay on Wye
Feb' '02

Trouble started on February 27th with the burning to death by a Muslim mob of 58 Hindu pilgrims, many of them women and children, returning by train from Ayodhya to their homes in Gujarat, a rich western state. That atrocity triggered worse: revenge killings of Muslims by Hindu mobs, especially in Gujarat's commercial capital, Ahmedabad. More than 600 people have so far died. 9.3.02

Not a pariah, a frien

KIPLING'S INDIAN FICTION

Kipling's Indian Fiction

Mark Paffard

© Mark Paffard 1989

All rights reserved. No reproduction, copy or transmission of this publication may be made without written permission.

No paragraph of this publication may be reproduced, copied or transmitted save with written permission or in accordance with the provisions of the Copyright Act 1956 (as amended), or under the terms of any licence permitting limited copying issued by the Copyright Licensing Agency, 33–4 Alfred Place, London WC1E 7DP.

Any person who does any unauthorised act in relation to this publication may be liable to criminal prosecution and civil claims for damages.

First published 1989

Published by
THE MACMILLAN PRESS LTD
Houndmills, Basingstoke, Hampshire RG21 2XS
and London
Companies and representatives
throughout the world

Printed in Hong Kong

British Library Cataloguing in Publication Data

Paffard, Mark, 1955–
   Kipling's Indian Fiction.
   1. English literature. Kipling, Rudyard,
   1865–1936. Influence of India
   I. Title
   828'.809

ISBN 0–333–46469–9

Contents

List of Plates	vii
Preface	ix
Acknowledgements	xii
Note on the Text	xiii
1 A British View of India	1
2 Early Stages	31
3 Soldiers in India	56
4 Illustrating the Native Feature	80
5 Kipling and the Eighteen-Nineties	103
Conclusions	128
Select Bibliography	135
Appendix	136
Notes and References	139
Index	146

List of Plates

1. 'Ready!' from *Punch*, 4 April 1885
2. 'Mary Winchester' from *Cassell's Illustrated History of India*, 2, p. 389
3. 'Caste' from *Punch*, 18 October 1890
4. 'Hands Off!' from *Punch*, 9 February 1889
5. 'The Burmese Toad' from *Punch*, 31 October 1885
6. Kipling's 'dream-map' from 'The Brushwood Boy', *Country Magazine*, December 1895
7. 'Kipling' by F. Attwood, from *Overheard in Arcady* by Robert Bridges, p. 67. (1895)
8. 'Kipling and Britannia' by Max Beerbohm, from *Poet's Corner* (1910)

Preface

This study deals not so much with a homogenous body of work by Kipling as with the influence of India on his writing. By the last quarter of the nineteenth century the British public already possessed their own mental image of India, and Kipling was very much part of a popular tradition as well as its greatest exponent. Of course, the Raj had to exist in the first place, and Kipling's first-hand experience is essential to his work, but the meanings that the tradition was attaching to India are the field that Kipling takes over and seeks, at times, to modify.

The tradition itself continues well into the twentieth century. In the last few years it has been revived both by a renewed interest in Kipling and by the appearance on film and television of the work of E. M. Forster and Paul Scott. If the political contours of old empires, and with them much of the vocabulary of the Victorian 'sahib', have changed forever, there are also continuities. The fear of rape, for example, is an extraordinarily durable theme. The sleuth-like historian who pieces together the story in Paul Scott's *The Jewel in the Crown* represents an approach to India that is indebted to Kipling and others. Its premise is that India is a land of mirages, in which only the most painstaking Western methods have the power to uncover the facts. It is basic, or 'latent', attitudes of this sort with which I am concerned in Kipling's case, for they have much light to shed on the shape his work took and the way in which it has been received. In this respect I obviously owe a great deal to Edward Said's *Orientalism*, and I would be pleased to think of this book as a small contribution to the project he has outlined.

The British view of India is, however, a particular application of the more general ideas and assumptions with which that society lived. Allowing for the importance of India as his subject, it is in the context of his period that I hope to have placed Kipling. The nineties are the years of his 'Indian Fiction'. After his most sustained account in *Kim* (1901), Kipling never turned to India again, and although he also wrote much that was not about India in that decade, its condition and future were his deepest preoccupations. Taking the first appearance of Kipling's work in England in 1888 as my starting point, I am concerned with the development of his style along with his treatment of India, and with the literary and historical context in which this took place.

Kipling's choice of words has been both celebrated and criticised for its precision. Vernon Lee in *The Handling of Words* (1912) made a formidable attack on the lack of fluidity and grace and the sense of authorial omnipresence that this style entails; but for all her focus on language she was too close to Kipling the belligerent imperialist to see this precision as anything but a symptom of narrow-mindedness. While Kipling's style obviously stems from the rigorous craftsmanship practised by his father and the Kipling family's pre-Raphaelite associates its individual mouldings are, I believe, formed by pressures and anxieties that show through the apparently unequivocal and often didactic surface of his stories. To find Kipling's outlook a grim one is not at all new, and where the critics have ever differed on this it has been mostly a matter of degree. My preference for a word like 'desperation' over the more dignified 'stoicism' is not meant to deny that Kipling sometimes expressed stoical views. I wonder, however, whether the writer who tells 'The Comforters', in the poem of that name, 'I never bothered you at all,/For God's sake go away!' has quite the reserve of the out-and-out Stoic.

In the nineties, as imperialism entered a more self-conscious phase, the public required just the sense of purpose that Kipling seemed to provide. Less providentially for him, it was a decade in which the whole pattern of social life was felt to be changing rapidly. His work epitomises a conflict between the artist's desire to meet the strange and unfamiliar on its own terms, and the need also to celebrate the familiar and comforting. If his choice was for the latter, he still experienced the conflict acutely both in India and in London. But however intense he may be, one can never escape from the fact that he actively believed both in the need to discriminate in all areas of life, and in having fairly simple rules by which to do so.

Described against this background, Kipling may appear a less commanding figure than either the one who has provoked so much harsh criticism or the one who emerges from two biographies and from J. M. S. Tompkins' classic study *The Art of Rudyard Kipling*. I do not think, however, that his work can or should become a less controversial matter, or that this can be entirely separated from the pleasure it gives. Some of his prejudices are typical of his period, but his conservatism has some sharp edges that cannot be removed by historical understanding, and I am sure many people in Britain today still like to think of themselves as 'British' in a way that resonates with his ideas and assumptions.

It is with due emphasis on the fact that the book's faults are my own doing entirely that I most gratefully acknowledge the advice and encouragement of Ian Small at every stage of its composition. His suggestions have been invaluable from start to finish. More than they know, I have relied on the support of the family and friends who have had to put up with Kipling as well as with me.

MARK PAFFARD
January 1988

Acknowledgements

Of the illustrations in this book, plates one, three, four and five are reproduced by permission of *Punch*, and the cartoon by Max Beerbohm by permission of Mrs Eva Reichmann. I am grateful to them, and also to the *Kipling Journal* and its editor for permission to re-use my article on 'Ortheris' from Volume 58, No. 230 (June 1984). The task of examining uncollected reviews of Kipling and other material on him was made much easier by the access granted me by John Burt to the Wimpole Hall archive at Sussex University, and to the Kipling Society's library at the Royal Commonwealth Society. My thanks to all concerned.

Note on the Text

In quoting from Kipling's work, I have not specified a particular edition. This is not an unknown practice; the reason being that the only truly comprehensive edition, the Sussex, is a rather rare and expensive item. Story titles, and chapter numbers (in brackets, following quotations) in the case of his few longer works, therefore have to suffice for identification, but readers requiring the volume in which a story is collected will find this information in the *Appendix*. The few abbreviations in the chapter references are self-explanatory, and the most frequent can be checked against the bibliography.

1
A British View of India

When Rudyard Kipling had his first stories published in England, took up residence in London, and quickly became one of the most widely acclaimed new authors ever, his reading public were more interested in the country he wrote about than they had ever been. At the start of the eighteen-nineties India dominated a British Empire that was at the height of its popularity in the mother country. Kipling's first readers in Britain felt that, through his stories, they were gaining a tremendous insight into Indian life. His work may have surprised and even shocked them at times, but the main effect of his stories was to supply a wealth of illustration to the generally rather vague ideas about India that they possessed. It is this awareness, rather than Kipling's personal history, that is described in this chapter. The British view of India – the common ground between Kipling and his readers – is the starting point from which he sought not only to inform his audience, but to persuade, entertain and offer his personal vision to them. India's remoteness from everyday experience offered unusual opportunities to a story-writer, just as its political and cultural importance imposed certain restraints. It thus forms a set of pressures and limits within the wider margins of the changing but still predominantly Victorian society for which Kipling wrote.

India at this time was very much the 'jewel in the crown' of British self-confidence, which had been nurtured by economic ascendancy and relative political stability since the Napoleonic wars. In some quarters at least it was a bellicose confidence, sharply hostile towards other colonisers, and especially towards Russia. The term 'jingoism' had its origins in a music-hall song of the 1880s, at a time of tension over Afghanistan:

We don't want to fight, but, by jingo! if we do,
We've got the ships, we've got the men, we've got the money too.[1]

.Britain's economic strength, based on coal and steel, was declining from the 1870s onwards against competition from

America and Germany; but what the public saw was the enlargement of the Empire as it became prudent for Britain to take direct control of its overseas markets. The same situation helped to spur a new wave of colonial expansion, notably in southern Africa, in the eighties and nineties, and while this was the work of individuals rather than statesmen, governments did little to impose restraint. In one famous case, when Gladstone attempted to disown General Gordon's manoeuvres in the Sudan in 1884, it was the government that lost face. 'Chinese' Gordon, already a *cause célèbre* before Khartoum, became a hero on whom death in a place beyond the reach of western civilisation conferred the status of instant legend. It was a legend bound up with the false glamour of the period, and a fitting target for the sceptical portraiture of Lytton Strachey's *Eminent Victorians.*

Britain's far-flung empire was both the scene of such vicarious adventure and a literal repository for the younger or more wayward sons of the ruling class. As *the* colony, the oldest and largest, India had a more substantial presence as a political entity. The British in India, the 'Anglo-Indians', complained vociferously that they were misrepresented and misunderstood in Britain, but not that they were ignored. The creation of the Indian Civil Service, a vast bureaucratic machine, and of related civic and cultural institutions in which at least the higher positions were occupied by Europeans, as well as an army with a fixed proportion of white soldiers, gave British families from all classes of society Indian connections. For the middle classes there was the prospect of a social rank unobtainable at home. India, too, was synonymous with the 'Raj'. Since 1877 Victoria had been both Queen of Britain and Empress of India; a conception whose popularity she herself was keen to foster. The Indian uprising or Mutiny of 1857 had been taken as proof that the Indians were barbaric people whom it was a heroic duty to rule and civilise, while India's North-West Frontier was the classical locus for the defence of civilisation against another kind of barbarism, that of the mighty Russian Empire. Every educated Briton had an idea of the vastness of India, of its hostile climate, and of the lives of his countrymen lost or broken in order to bring it under British rule. Few if any doubted that the introduction of education in English after Macaulay's famous minute of 1839, the building of a railway system, and the introduction of a modified form of Western government constituted a comprehensive and beneficial civilisation of the country. India, with its tiger drawing

Britannia's chariot in harness with the lion, could present the British with a flattering picture of themselves. (Plate 1)

The abstract notion of India and Britain working harmoniously in tandem had its counterpart in the official doctrine that India would eventually be governed by Indians; but in practice the doctrine was a dead letter, and the British self-image drew much of its strength from a radically unflattering view of 'natives'. This is well illustrated by the comments of two of the most influential and prolific Victorian intellectuals, John Ruskin and Thomas Carlyle. In 1849 Carlyle was addressing the 'Nigger Question' as he perceived it in Jamaica, and his notes of intemperance and self-admiration can be found echoing down the rest of the century.

> Far over the sea we have a few black persons rendered extremely "free" indeed. Sitting yonder with their beautiful muzzles up to the ears in pumpkins, imbibing sweet pulps and juices; the grinder and incisor teeth ready for ever new work, and the pumpkins cheap as grass in those rich climates: while the sugar-crops rot around them uncut, because labour cannot be hired, so cheap are the pumpkins. . . . Under the soil of Jamaica, before it could even produce spices, or any pumpkins, the bones of many thousand British men had to be laid. Brave Colonel Fortescue, brave Colonel Sedgwick, brave Colonel Brayne – the dust of many strong old English hearts lies there; worn down swiftly in frightful travail, chaining the Devils, which were manifold.

However often Kipling returns to the question of the 'balance-sheet' of Empire, his onesidedness at least never exceeds this. Ruskin, in 1858, was writing in the wake of the Mutiny, so that his remarks have topicality, although their occasion is a lecture on art.

> We are thus urged naturally to inquire what is the effect on the moral character in each nation, of this vast difference in their pursuits and apparant capacities? and whether those rude chequers of the tartan, or the exquisitely fancied involutions of the Cashmere, fold habitually over the noblest hearts. . . . Out of the peat cottage come faith, courage, self-sacrifice, purity and piety, and whatever else is fruitful in the work of heaven; out of the ivory palace come treachery, cruelty, cowardice, idolatry, bestiality – whatever else is fruitful in the work of Hell.[2]

Against the huge output of both men these comments are, of course, mere asides. Ruskin and Carlyle were no more deeply interested in the processes of colonial expansion than were the British in general. There was in fact complete popular ignorance, in every western power, both of the conditions of life in Africa and the Orient and of the real reasons for being there. In Britain the idea of an empire was regarded with suspicion for a long time, as something unpleasantly autocratic. No-one admired the Second Empire of Napoleon III in France, and Charles Dilke in his *Greater Britain* (1868) dismissed 'a mere imperialism, where one man rules and the rest are slaves'. Gladstone declared in 1880 that the foundations of the British Empire in India could ill bear examination. But the laissez-faire approach of Liberal governments, coupled with public apathy, could not turn back the tide set in motion by Disraeli, who had declared that 'The East is a career'.[3] Meanwhile the entrepreneurs of empire flourished, and Conservative governments could not check them either. Cecil Rhodes thrust his way north through Africa by disregarding protocol. Kipling, who was to become his friend and associate, was much annoyed by the public's apparent indifference to the work of the empire-builders, and expressed it sharply in poems like 'The English Flag', while he responded to liberal criticism with vituperation. Politically, however, the imperialists had won the day and were given economic backing. Naval expenditure doubled from £10 million in 1875 to £20 million in 1895, and would double again before the First World War.[4] In the first half of the nineties indifference was at least gilded over by the enthusiasm of the press. These were the years both of the Kipling 'boom' and of the first wave of mass-circulation journals and newspapers. Victoria's Golden Jubilee had fixed the idea of an empire on which the sun never set in the public mind, and her Diamond Jubilee was already aproaching. Writing of the moment at which Kipling's work began to appear in England, Holbrook Jackson recalled that 'when Kitchener "avenged" the death of Gordon, and obliterated the failures of Wolseley in Egypt, by defeating the Mahdi at Omdurman, and retaking Khartoum, slumbering Imperialism awoke with a strange and arrogant light in its eyes.'[5]

There is a distinction, although it would be tiresome to make it on every occasion, between the way in which India affected the British and the way in which they 'affected' India. Away from the sonorities of Carlyle and Ruskin the latter attitude contains an element of real affectation and voyeurism, and it is with this that I am most concerned since Kipling's work by its very nature caters for it. By dwelling on particular topics, by tailoring India to the destinies of his protagonists, he inevitably reinvents it as a spectacle, quite irrespective of how solidly he reflects the 'internal', Anglo-Indian view. In his pioneering book *Orientalism*, Edward Said distinguishes between the 'latent' and 'manifest' approaches of the West to the East. The set of unconscious assumptions that make up latent orientalism include 'the separateness of the Orient, its eccentricity, its backwardness, its feminine penetrability, its supine malleability'. As a result, 'every writer on the Orient, from Renan to Marx (ideologically speaking) or from the most rigorous scholars (Lane and Sacy) to the most powerful imaginations (Flaubert and Nerval) saw the Orient as a locale requiring Western attention, reconstruction, even redemption.'[6] Said's emphasis is on the literary and academic appropriation of the Orient, and at the level of popular culture the 'manifest' depiction is often little more than a vehicle for 'latent' prejudice. In addition Britain's long domination of India throws up many stereotyped embodiments of latent orientalism, which may be frozen into contradictory shapes. The ubiquitous native servant is, on the one hand, inscrutable, sinister, and lecherous, but also naive, childlike and subservient. It then becomes difficult to depict the sinister type without inadvertently putting in some detail that coincides with the buffoon, and indeed a comic repulsiveness is a feature of oriental villainy that eventually finds itself at home in the comics and cartoon-strips of the twentieth century. Since, in its Victorian manifestations, attention is really focused on the desires, fears, and irritations of the white observer – on the Britishness that compasses and deals equally with India – such incongruity passes unnoticed.

This British self-regard is captured in an illustration to *Cassell's Illustrated History of India*, entitled 'Portrait of Mary Winchester, Captive of the Lushais'.[7] Mary Winchester, we learn from a footnote (despite the portrait her story is hardly a major event in Indian history), was captured and then released by a tribe on India's north-eastern borders at the age of seven. The fact that her life was preserved while her beautiful curls were cut off and kept as a memento clearly implies to the author that she became a temporary deity, and perhaps that this is not an unnatural position for a white girl among savages. She looks out of her portrait with a forceful expression that seems to derive more from the busts of Roman emperors than from the usual Victorian conventions. The two-volume *Illustrated History* by James Grant was published in 1877, the year of Victoria's official adoption of the title of Empress of India. It is considerably bulkier than those appearing towards the end of the century, and its double columns of print incorporate lengthy quotations from earlier historians, official pronouncements, and leaders from *The Times*. Grant himself was primarily a prolific novelist, whose list of titles, from *Adventures of an Aide-de-Camp* to *Fairer than a Fairy* give some idea of his place in the book market. His career also included much military experience, and involvement with the Scottish 'Jacobite' movement, but he was not known as an expert on Indian history. Ostensibly middlebrow and monumental at the same time, the book gives an immediate sense of Britain's relationship with the newly formed Raj.

This relationship owed its existence to the Indian 'Mutiny' of 1857, which had led to the inception of direct rule over India, with all that that implied. It had meant a greater formal recognition of the rights of Indians who, as subjects of the Queen, could not be left without some degree of formal education and relief from famine, although the East India Company had, with increasing political supervision, been undertaking such duties already. There was also a new ceremonial element, again adopting traditions well-established, culminating in the proclamation of the Queen-Empress, the great Delhi durbar attended by the Prince of Wales, and the change of the Governor-General's title to that of Viceroy. But these changes were of far less significance than the great awakening of interest in, and simultaneous reaction against, India and Indians that the Mutiny aroused. It was immediately and from then on perceived as, in the popular phrase, the 'Epic of the Race'. It created a distrust and dislike of 'natives', and a withdrawal from all but official and the most superficial contact with them that was to last, sometimes with increased intensity, as long as the Raj itself. In *A Passage to India* Ronny believes that 'We're not here to be pleasant' adequately sums up the role of the British official, and a colleague remarks that the Mutiny records should be the white man's bible in India. There was no time at which the spectre of the Mutiny was not an effective weapon on the side of opposition to political change. The 1904 edition of Murray's handbook still devotes the longest, final section of its introduction to a detailed account of the uprising.[8] Tourists would want to re-live an event whose immediate impact had been assessed as follows:

Of the effect these stories had at home we find Macaulay writing thus: "The cruelties of the sepoys have inflamed the nation to a degree unprecedented within my memory. Peace Societies, Aborigine Protection Societies, and Societies for the Reformation of Criminals, are silenced. There is one terrible cry for revenge! The account of that dreadful military execution at Peshawur – forty men blown at once from the mouths of cannon, their heads, legs, and arms flying in all directions – was read with delight by people who three months ago were against all capital punishment."[9]

The almost universal belief in innate racial characteristics, to be rendered more 'scientific' by Social Darwinism, meant that the traits of character that Indians were considered to possess – these almost invariably being effeteness, sloth, barbarism, and cunning – had to be regarded as fixed quantities. From the British point of view the natives thus stood condemned by the Mutiny for all time, both past and future. Grant, for example, introduces the subject by remarking that' "The first and most vivid impression received from the pages of early travellers in India", says a writer, "is made by the frequent recurrence of premeditated cruelty". As they were in the days of Mandeville and Marco Polo, so were the Hindostanees in the days of the mutiny in their lust of cruelty and bloodshed.'[10] John Lawrence, Lieutenant–Governor of the Punjab at the time, and later a rather ineffectual viceroy, described it as a struggle 'between Christianity and civilisation on one side and barbarism and heathenism on the other.' His words are still the final authority for T. W. Holderness in *Peoples and Problems of India* in 1913, encapsulating for the *Home University Library of Modern Knowledge* the received ideas of previous decades.

The Mutiny was apparently sparked off by the suspected use of cow or pork fat to grease the cartridges of the new Enfield rifles. British officers exacerbated the situation, especially at Meerut, near Delhi, by severely punishing sepoys (Indian soldiers) who would not use the rifle. Neither Grant nor J. Talboys Wheeler, whose *College History of India* (1888) is a model of scholastic brevity, accept this as an explanation.[11] Both conclude that the sepoys had become pampered and lost their discipline, and had seized the opportunity given them by lack of European oversight. If the natives in general had grievances they could be characterised as reactionary – fear of loss of caste as traditional village life was threatened by the advent of the railways, resistance to the attempted suppression of suttee (the immolation of a widow with her dead husband) and to modifications in the system of land tenure. The westernisation of India, including the annexation of the kingdom of Oudh (whose capital, Lucknow, became a focal point of the rebellion), was being aggressively pushed forward by the Governor-General, Lord Dalhousie. However only R. W. Frazer in *British India* (Unwin's 'Story of the Nations' series, 1898) sees this as a factor, and says bluntly of the greased cartridges episode that 'the whole edifice of folly was crowned with a stupendous blunder, fraught with fatal consequences.'[12] The general belief that the mutiny was indeed primarily a military revolt is not shared by modern historians, but is perhaps explained by the conviction that the Indian peasant was totally oblivious to his rulers. Frazer, for example, tells us that 'From time immemorial the husbandmen in the rich river valleys of India have ploughed their lands, sown the seed, and reaped the produce calmly, indifferent to the coming and going of their foreign rulers.'[13] It is this belief that informs a very early verse of Kipling's, whose sentiments at first glance seem unusual by comparison with the humorous Anglo-Indian 'ditties' among which it appears.

> And the Ploughman settled the share
> More deep in the sun-dried clod:-
> "Moghul, Mahratta, and *Mlech*, from the North,
> "And White Queen over the Seas -
> "God raiseth them up and driveth them forth
> "As the dust of the ploughshare flies in the breeze;
> "But the wheat and the cattle are all my care,
> "And the rest is the will of God."
>
> ('What the People Said')

This outlook received encouragement as Dalhousie's policies were quickly recognised as part of the problem in government circles. His successor, Canning, was quick to grant an amnesty and to take measures which would bring the land-owners and leaders of Indian society into sympathy with the British. India was positively encouraged to think of itself as a feudal society. Several decades after the Mutiny we still find the rising, westernised middle class that would eventually lead India to independence subjected to an exceptionally strong barrage of dislike and ridicule. A novel about the Mutiny by an Anglo-Indian, Flora Annie Steel's *On the Face of the Waters*, also points to British mismanagement, and condemns the sentences of six to ten years handed out to sepoys at Meerut. It also records that some white refugees found shelter in Indian villages, but the novel still plays on the emotive theme of the white woman's vulnerability to rape or murder, and offers no reassessment of the scale of atrocities committed by the rebels and the British executioners who blew them from the mouths of cannon.[14] The feelings recorded by one of the British soldiers fighting against the sepoys could, one feels, be summoned up by any Anglo-Indian for the next fifty years at least.

> "Our blood is roused", wrote one of them at this time; "we have seen friends, relations, mothers, wives and children brutally murdered and their bodies mutilated frightfully. This alone, without the pluck that made us victorious over the Russians, would enable us, with God's assistance, to be victorious over these enemies. As the riflemen charge – ten to a hundred – the word is passed, 'Remember the ladies! Remember the babies!' and everything flies before them. Hundreds are shot down or bayoneted. The sepoys, it is true, fight like demons; but we are British and they are natives."[15]

Natives are invariably regarded as one degree less courageous than any white troops. Kipling, though he occasionally pays a victor's tribute to the fighting spirit of some Orientals, as in the poem 'Fuzzy-Wuzzy', goes into this with some precision when Private Mulvaney declares that the white soldiers who took Lungtunpen from the Burmese stark naked would take St Petersburg in their drawers.[16] His fiction echoes the Mutiny when it plays on the vulnerability of European women or children, on feelings of outrage and revenge towards natives, but chiefly by sustaining the possibility of unpredictable violence. Only the animal story 'The Undertakers' is actually set against the background of the Mutiny, but there is no reference to names or places. There are only the waves of corpses on which the old crocodile feasts as they come down the river Ganges. It is a well-worked parable of Indian barbarism – ignorance, lust and gluttony – set against the inevitable white superiority. When the white men shoot the crocodile at the end of his tale the Indian villagers are rescued from the image of their former selves. As such it forms an interesting link between Kipling's early work about Anglo-Indian and native life and the apparently mellower works with an element of fantasy – chiefly the *Jungle Books* and *Kim*.

The establishment of direct rule certainly brought about a change of emphasis. It was now widely understood that Britain held India for the benefit of Indians. The administrative machinery grew and prided itself on its efficiency, and the standard of justice dispensed by district officials undoubtedly improved. Emily Eden, who saw India in the entourage of her brother, the governor-general Lord Auckland, had observed in 1839 that 'It is horrible to think how this class of Europeans oppresses the natives . . . the poor natives cannot really understand that they are no longer under their own despotic chiefs. They will be a long time learning it here.' She was describing the local magistrates. Lord Canning believed that the European community in 1861 was 'very small, very ignorant of and indifferent to India, and very selfish.'[17] After the Mutiny India was to be governed more dispassionately, but with an emphasis on duty that implied distaste for its subjects. At best Indians remained a pliable, lumpen mass – an attitude liable to defeat the proclaimed intention of educating them; as it was liable, with Kipling, to defeat his insistence that the British should learn to know them better. With the influx of government servants white women also arrived in India in numbers for the first time. The 'memsahib' was a new source of friction, for her very presence helped to keep up the echoes of the Mutiny. Denied the social pastimes of wives in England, frequently absent from their husbands, and left with little to do but supervise domestic servants, memsahibs became notorious for their mixture of arrogance and nervous irritability. A second unwelcome addition from the Indian point of view was the reinforcement of the white contingent of the British army, now to be maintained as a third of its total. The working-class soldiers of whom Kipling wrote could regard themselves as the superior of any Indian, and they too were bored. Given the racial attitudes of their superiors it is hardly surprising that their resort to pugilism or the regimental brothel spilled over into incidents of assault and rape against the native population which the authorities did little to check.

'You will soon find that the more you are down on them the better they will respect you', a fellow-private in India told Frank Richards in 1906, and added, speaking of the most regal of India's viceroys, 'Old Curzon is no damned good, this country wants a Viceroy who will keep the bleeding natives down.'[18] Here is the always noticeable difference between the view of the ordinary British citizen and the loftier aspirations of Queen Victoria and her ministers. Many educated Anglo-Indians, Kipling among them, got to know and respect individual 'natives', but every white Victorian unhesitatingly described Indians in general as 'black' men. A clear example is provided by Colonel Creighton, the ostensible expert on Indian ethnography, in Chapter 7 of *Kim*. Kipling's readers, a little more detached than the soldier but no more able to question the fundamental separateness and backwardness of the Orient, might well have known as much about Indians as Holderness provides in this paragraph.

> If during a long journey he observes the population of the railway stations, he will notice a change in type. The change is very gradual, but in the course of twelve hours quite noticeable. If he makes a stay at a place and should pass different sections of the inhabitants under review, he will notice marked physical differences of colour, build, stature, shape of head, features, hair. At one end of the scale is the Brahman, with light complexion and almost European type of face and build; at the other the swarthy squat form of the coolie in the streets.[19]

Perhaps the first widely read writer to say something about individual castes and creeds and to stress the tremendous variety of peoples is Kipling in *Kim* (1901). From Holderness there emerge two ways of classifying Indians; either as Northern or Southern, or of high or low caste.

The races of the north are the 'proud and warlike' Afghans and Sikhs; those of the south are servile, Dravidian (negroid) rather than Aryan, and find occupation either as coolies or beggars. It is the highest castes – Rajahs and other independent rulers and Brahmins (the priest caste) – and secondarily northerners in general, who approximate most closely to the white man: 'The lower the caste the nearer does its type come to the blackness and stumpy figure of the Dravidian.' The Aryans who invaded India from the north and founded the Mughal dynasty are compared to the Norsemen and Normans of Europe. Holderness also notes that 'The invaders averted complete amalgamation with the inferior race by taking women but not giving them. They behaved in fact towards the Dravidians whom they conquered in exactly the same way as some planters in America behaved to the African slaves whom they imported.'[20] The precedent before the English Aryan in India could scarcely be more obvious, although in official circles it was strictly frowned upon, particularly in Curzon's time. It is a theme of several of Kipling's stories, and clearly had a strong effect on his readers. Francis Adams in 1891 took Kipling to task for his 'rows of Anglo-Indian bachelors of all sorts . . . inspiring dark-eyed little native girls with dog-like adorations.'[21] Others were more enthusiastic. One respect in which Kipling appears to take an unconventional line, in for example the story 'His Private Honour' and in references to the abandoned novel 'Mother Maturin', is in his acceptance of mixed marriage and of an increased Eurasian population as an inevitable part of his political vision of a semi-independent India permanently settled by the British.

The preference for the 'Aryan' type of native was reinforced by the fact that the northern races of India were also predominantly Muslim rather than Hindu. In a period when the British took pride in being a belligerent civilisation is was easy for them to identify to some extent with the warlike faith of Islam. Richard Burton, the famous traveller, even made the scandalous assertion that it was better suited to some regions of the world than Christianity. Kipling sums up a widespread attitude, and certainly one that runs through much of his own writing when he remarks that 'I have never met an Englishman who hated Islam as I have met Englishmen who hated some other faiths . . . where there are Mohammedans there is a comprehensible civilisation.'[22] Discrimination in favour of the Mohammedan is of course hemmed in by the fact that he necessarily falls into the wider caregories of 'native' and 'heathen'. He may, however, unlike most Hindus, make a good soldier. Although the Mutiny took the restoration of the Muslim Mughal dynasty as a rallying point, it is almost invariably to 'Hindoos' that Grant refers when he has an unpleasant generalisation to make. It comes as no surprise to find one or two admiring portraits of Muslim Lahore. The tropical southern part of India, with its high incidence of cholera and famine, was naturally less congenial to the British. For precisely that reason it contributed more to their mental landscape, as Kipling was well aware. As his heroes travel south from the Punjab on famine-relief duty in 'William the Conqueror' he describes 'an India more strange to them than to the untravelled Englishman – the flat, red India of palm-tree, palmyra-palm and rice, the India of the picture-books, of *Little Henry and his Bearers* – all dead and dry in the baking heat.'[23]

The best to be said of its population according to Holderness is that their religious and mental outlook is one of resigned pessimism and quiet melancholy. Bengal, in the south-east, was also the home of the western–educated native, the Hindu 'babu', who comes in for an endless stream of abuse from Anglo-Indians who felt their positions threatened by the rise into the administration of a section of the native population. The babu, in popular misconception, was an unprincipled, cowardly creature, who spoke a grotesque version of English full of malapropisms. At the end of 1895 the distinguished Anglo-Indian administrator Sir William Wilson Hunter was writing to protest about the distorted picture given by *Punch's* 'Specimens of Babuese' – a fair indication of their familiarity as a type.[24] Hindu journals and the nascent Indian National Congress, founded in 1888, were related targets for disgruntled Anglo-Indian opinion.

This, then, represents the variety of Indians as Kipling's readers, or at least some of them, would have known it. We can probably add some indistinct knowledge of particular races, particularly those who often served in the army – the Sikhs, the Gurkhas, and the Mahrattas of Southern India, and of the Burmese, whose country had only recently been annexed in its entirety – as well as an acquaintance with the main tenets of Buddhism, especially the transmigration of souls. But the perceived gulf between white men and any kind of 'native' puts such knowledge as there may have been into a rather distant perspective. John Lockwood Kipling, Rudyard's father, who was an authority on Indian arts and crafts, still speaks impartially throughout his book *Beast and Man in India* (1893) of 'natives'. Of parrots, for example, he remarks that 'It is seldom a bird in native hands speaks well. Orientals are easily contented, and, though they can take pains in some matters, are inclined to think that parrot speech comes, as Dogberry said of reading and writing, by nature.'[26] The 'Dogberry' view of Indians should be noted, for Kipling exploits it to great effect in *Kim*. Lockwood Kipling was a rare champion of traditional Indian art against the prevailing tendency to teach Indian students by European methods and models, but otherwise he shows no inclination to diverge from an occidental set of values.[27] The mechanical repetition of similes in Indian poetry is explained, for example, by the banality of the Indian mind. His book, with its chapter on each animal, is obviously written to entertain, but it also has a thesis. It undertakes to show that Lecky's favourable view of oriental religions in his famous *History of European Morals from Constantine to Charlemagne* (1869) is mistaken in that the Buddhistic peoples who do not actually kill animals nevertheless tend to treat them abominably while they are still alive. For all Lockwood Kipling's evident charm he has the characteristic Victorian tendency to smug seriousness.

He is by no means the only writer in whom the attempt at a humane outlook is checked by a sense of unquestionable racial superiority. Thus, the belief in universal education that James Grant professes when his eye is on the broad sweep of Empire tends to vanish when confronted by particulars: 'One effect of the spread of education has been to teach the ryots (peasants) to take care of themselves, and, allowing for physical and moral differences, to become as intractable as the same class in other countries.'[28] The stock response that was evolved to deal with the educated Hindu lays stress on his *mere* education, while it is the white man who acts. We can hear an identical tone of dismissive flippancy in the two comments below:

> Over cow-byres of unimaginable impurity you may hear young students debating politics and local self-government with that love of wordy abstractions and indifference to practical considerations which have always been marks of the Hindu. (1893)

> As the golf habit has fastened upon middle-aged and elderly persons in England, so the conference-going habit has settled upon the educated Indian community. As a form of recreation the conference is not without its merits in an eastern climate. (1913)[29]

Another frequent tactic is to assert that the assimilation of western ways is not more than skin deep. That the Indian is not to be trusted under any circumstances, and that his lascivious nature, sufficiently demonstrated by the customs of child-marriage and polygamy, is a particular threat to white women, is a recurring theme of Anglo-Indian fiction. In much of Kipling's work the white man is firmly in control and, except in his stories of Simla life, the memsahib is wisely kept out of the picture. The common theme of potential rape is relegated to one absurd children's story, 'Wee Willie Winkie', in which the six-year-old hero defends a white woman from Afghan tribesmen. Stories like 'The Return of Imray' show natives behaving with unpredictable and cold-blooded savagery, although Kipling is way ahead of many of his contemporaries in having some understanding of their behaviour.

Clearly the production of an image of the typical Indian as lecherous and treacherous, a half-naked, irresponsible barbarian until disciplined by the British, but still fundamentally ungrateful and unreliable, was governed by the white community's own insistence on a state of de facto apartheid, which had reached its height by the 1880s. It could well be argued that an English reader of Emily Eden's *Up the Country*, which describes her travels through India in the Governor-General's procession of 1839, would obtain a more balanced view than an Anglo-Indian actually living the prescribed life on station fifty years later. The Hon. Emily, at any rate, did not respond with terror, even when confronted with real 'fakeers'. To her they are 'the most horrid-looking monsters it is possible to see. They never wear any clothes, but powder themselves all over with white or yellow powder, and put red streaks over their faces. They look like the raw material of so many Grimaldis.'[30] *Up the Country* was published in 1866, and some of her later Victorian readers may have been surprised by her casual report that 'We dined with Colonel J yesterday. He lives, I believe, quite in the native style, with a few black Mrs J's gracing his domestic circle when we are not here.'[31] Such a lifestyle had become increasingly taboo for officers of any rank, though it enjoyed a brief resurgence in Burma after its annexation in 1885. Sexuality, and its connection with property, was of course a matter of deep concern to society in general. Ronald Pearsall's *The Worm in the Bud* gives a detailed account of attitudes to sex at all levels of Victorian society, while Fraser Harrison's *The Dark Angel* studies some of its consequences in literature. The fear of any promiscuity on the part of respectable women was intensified by the fear that illegitimate children might gain access to the property of the upper classes, as the furore in Britain over the Married Women's Property Acts revealed. Thus racial mixes, doubtless immoral if the father was white and the mother black, had sound reasons for being regarded with horror if a white woman bore a black child. Perhaps rape by a black man was the commonest of bogeys under the Raj in part because it would be the only saving clause if the unthinkable actually happened. As far as India and the rest of the Empire were concerned there was an intimate connection between political and sexual domination, facets of which appear in literature of all kinds.

It was generally accepted that a man had the right to 'sow his wild oats'. The dramatist Pinero was breaking new ground and challenging his audience when he implicitly attacked this principle in *The Second Mrs Tanqueray* (1892). On the other hand Richard Le Gallienne, a considerable literary figure in the nineties, and by no means a blind adherent of Kipling or Imperialism, can only admire the words that Kipling puts into the mouth of his dying Empire-builder in 'The *Mary Gloster*':

> Mr Kipling has seldom done better than in the old man's last wandering speech, a remarkably outspoken statement of the whole morality of man:

> 'Mary, why didn't *you* warn me? I've allus heeded to you,
> Excep' – I know – about women; but you are a spirit now;
> An' wife, they was only women, and I was a man. That's how.
> An' a man 'e must go with a woman, as you *could* not understand;
> But I never talked 'em secrets. I paid 'em out o' hand.'[32]

To go to a prostitute or to keep a native woman was by no means uncommon in Kipling's India – as indeed it was not in England, where the high incidence of prostitution in Victorian times has been well-documented. Where Kipling has touched on this subject his manner has been somewhat beguiling to his critics. In 'Without Benefit of Clergy' and 'Beyond the Pale' he writes with sympathetic vividness of liaisons between white men and native women which have to be kept secret. In both stories we are nevertheless pressed to see the tragic ending as inevitable. The two white men in his fiction who enter openly into a marriage with a native woman do so because of particular circumstances – one is a subaltern in upper Burma, the other a tea–planter who will spend his entire life in India. More remarkably both the eponymous 'Georgie Porgie' and the tea-planter Phil Garron are portrayed as sentimentally shallow and uncaring individuals. In Phil Garron's case individual shortcomings and the decision to marry are entirely related:

> He was dropping all his English correspondents one by one, and beginning more and more to look on India as his home. Some men fall this way, and they are of no use afterwards. . . . He did what many planters have done before him – that is to say, he made up his mind to marry a Hill-girl and settle down. He was

seven-and-twenty then, with a long life before him, but no spirit to go through with it. So he married Dunmaya by the forms of the English church, and some fellow-planters said he was a fool, and some said he was a wise man.³³

If native woman represents a step down, she is nevertheless far more acceptable than native man. 'It is curious', Kipling remarks in the same story, 'to think that a Hill-man after a lifetime's education is a Hill-man still; but a Hill-woman can in six months master most of the ways of her English sisters.' The hill-people, or paharis, were unusual in not keeping women in the seclusion of purdah. On the other couple of occasions on which Kipling uses a hill-woman in 'Lispeth' and in *Kim* (they are in fact the same person), her function is to make advances to the white man. Examination reveals that Kipling studiously avoids fictional situations in which sexual behaviour could become a threat to the established system, though he frequently approaches in their direction. For example, by looking at his 'Love-o'-Women' (1893) in conjunction with the stories mentioned above, one may conclude that he will write about liaisons between white men and black women, or about prostitution, but not both together, though this was obviously the most commonplace situation of all.

The most striking thing to English eyes about the majority of oriental women was their strict seclusion, the wearing of the veil, and the possibility that an Indian husband's zenana might contain several wives. Lockwood Kipling regards these women with pity:

> It is not too fantastical to perceive in the Indian development of something like a separate language – *choti boli* – literally little talk, the clipped and childish speech of imprisoned women of starved intellect, an evidence of a great social disability.

but this is abruptly qualified by:

> Yet if the women of India have the faults of an exaggerated domesticity, they have also its qualities, and their estate should be understood before reformers rush to meddle with it.³⁴

Women, after all, were regarded as entirely different in nature from men in Victorian society. They were the property of their husbands, they could soothe and comfort but not act, and unless they betrayed and sullied their sex they were entirely chaste. A number of writers actually feel admiration for the complete loyalty involved in the Indian way of marriage, particularly as exemplified in the custom of suttee. Mrs Steel plays with the idea in *On the Face of the Waters*, and her attitude is openly expressed by Emily Eden when she hears of the suttee of the wives of the great ruler Runjit Singh:

> I begin to think that the 'hundred-wife' system is better than the one wife rule, they are more attached and faithful. . . . Those poor dear ranees whom we visited and thought so beautiful and so merry have actually burnt themselves . . . they were such gay young creatures, and they died with the most obstinate courage.[35]

The British had nevertheless been officially attempting to eradicate suttee since at least the 1830s. If this practice at least demonstrated conjugal fidelity, that of child-marriage was plainly symptomatic of nothing but the 'backwardness' of Indian society. Yet the striking feature of the *Punch* cartoon of 1890 (Plate 3), with its 'Child-wife or child-widow in agony kneeling' at the skirts of the motherly Britannia is the large and shapely bust of the child-wife, compared with the complete absence of the same in the depiction of Britannia. Whatever the overt message, any drawing of oriental woman is clearly too good an opportunity to miss, and this attitude progresses a stage further in the depiction of Samoa in a cartoon of 1889 (Plate 4) where the cartoonist has clearly seized the opportunity afforded by a dispute between two other colonial powers to draw a figure that might have shocked in almost any other circumstances. In the first cartoon the shadow of 'CASTE' hovers over the unfortunate woman, aptly summarising the negligible interest that the British really took in the Indian social system. Caste is just one more sympton of backwardness. 'How is it', asks Holderness, 'that while in Europe the family, the clan, and the tribe have been absorbed into the nation, in India they have solidified into cast-iron compartments into which the whole population is distributed and locked up?'[36] As if the British ever pretended that they wanted India to aspire to nationhood. At the same time the Anglo-Indians borrowed the word to apply to themselves, appropriately enough considering the hierarchical system of government that the Raj had evolved. Kipling is an excellent example of such usage – his borrowing having an extra dimension where soldiers are concerned, since the Indian of high caste was, historically speaking, a warrior.

The Englishman accustomed from his own folklore and poetry to the idea of the maiden locked away from the public gaze was undoubtedly excited by the discovery of a comparable situation in India, especially when he realised that oriental woman might nevertheless be more accessible, as not raising considerations of property, than a woman of his own race. It is obviously necessary to view the entire web of attitudes relating to Indian women in the context of Victorian sexual attitudes in Kipling's period, which was also that of the 'New Woman' in England, where novels like George Du Maurier's *Trilby* and Grant Allen's *The Woman Who Did* were presenting a more adventurous, rather than more genuinely independent stereotype. It was still very much the case, however, that women were the anchors of society, whose choice of marriage partner was an essential lever to the standards that men might be expected to set themselves. Since such leverage was naturally enhanced by youth and beauty a woman's ornamental quality was also important. Coventry Patmore, whose 'epic' of ordinary courtship and marriage seems to have expressed for the Victorians all that they held dear, puts it like this:

> Art and strange lands her pomp supply
> With purple, chrome, and cochineal,
> Ochre and lapis lazuli;
> The worm its golden woof presents;
> Whatever runs, flies, dives, or delves,
> All doff for her their ornaments,
> Which suit her better than themselves;
> And all, by this their power give,
> Proving her right to take, proclaim
> Her beauty's clear prerogative
> To profit so by Eden's Blame.[37]

It is interesting to see that Patmore's glorification involves in itself the necessity of tribute from strange lands, and offers what sounds like a covert justification ('their power to give/Proving her right to take') for imperial exploitation.

To the Victorian male every woman was to a certain extent shrouded in mystery. Although there was little enough reverence attached to Britain's possession of India, the idea of the sub-continent as a passive, female entity nevertheless reinforced the belief of most Anglo-Indians that India functioned according to her own natural law and rhythm, and that the intricacies of her social fabric were best left alone. Thus the work of missionaries was frequently deprecated as pointless or even dangerous. At best the Indian was incapable of understanding Christianity; at worst the reaction might be a second mutiny. If the Victorians associated their wives with images of purity and serenity they also imagined, especially in the latter half of the century, that women had a larger residue of primitive instinct and wanton cruelty. The same pre-Raphaelite studio in Cheyne Walk produced Rossetti's 'Beata Beatrix' and A. F. Sandys' 'Medea'.[38] Or as Kipling later put it in hackneyed form, 'The female of the species is more deadly than the male'. The Indian woman, usually invisible behind the purdah screen, thus epitomised that aspect of India with which it was dangerous to meddle. The fact that every large military cantonment in India had its Lal Bazaar, or brother, and its attendant Lock hospital for the treatment of syphilis could be ignored. The ordinary soldiers who used these facilities had no place in society themselves.

It was with equal determination that the Raj attempted to ignore its Eurasian population. In the eighteenth century Eurasians had been called 'Indo-Britons' and had been quite influential, but in the 1790s they were excluded from the commissioned ranks of the army and from the civil service. Under the Raj the typical Eurasian was a minor government official, cut off from the 'pukka' sahibs by his Portuguese origin and Roman Catholic religion, and regarded with little less aversion than the Muslim or Hindu who might fill a similar post. The most successful Eurasians practised medicine, but were restricted in this too by their exclusion from official circles. By the end of the century paranoia about racial mixes had become such that the Eurasian was assumed to have inherited only the characteristic vices of the two races from which he sprang. An Anglo-Indian novelist says precisely this in 1909, and so, under the guise of a transparently condescending interest, does Kipling twenty years earlier: 'The Black and the White mix very quaintly in their ways. Sometimes the White shows in spurts of fierce, childish pride – which is the Pride of Race run crooked – and sometimes the Black in still fiercer abasement and humility, half-heathenish customs and strange, unaccountable impulses to crime.'[39] The 'Pride of Race'! The assurance of white superiority is part of the syntax used to describe India, and racial 'contamination' is completely abhorrent. An article in the *Contemporary Review* (June 1888) spells this out: 'The chasm between the brown man and the white is unfathomable, has existed in all ages, and exists still everywhere. No white man marries a brown wife, no brown man marries a white wife, without an inner sense of having been false to some unintelligible but irresistible command.'[40] In 1885 Kipling began work on an ambitious novel to be entitled 'Mother Maturin'. In a letter he remarks that 'It's not one bit nice or proper but it carries a grim sort of moral with it and tries to deal with the unutterable horrors of lower class Eurasian and native life as they exist outside reports and reports and reports.' It would have been difficult to build a large-scale work around Eurasian characters, given the ingrained feelings about them. His parents advised him that it could only succeed if published in England, further from the actuality, but in any event 'Mother Maturin' disappeared without trace.[41]

What Kipling in fact published in the early part of his career were stories about native 'types', and stories about the British army in India, which will be considered in later chapters, and a considerable body of early writing about the Anglo-Indians themselves. Apart from his last, and in many ways most comprehensive account of the country in *Kim*, there is one novel set in India. This is the improbable pot-boiler *The Naulakha*, written in collaboration with Wolcott Balestier. The setting here is not British India but one of the semi-independent Indian states watched over by a British resident. Although a number of these states still existed they were a throwback to pre-Mutiny and pre-industrial days, when independent kingdoms were brought under British influence by treaty rather than by force. The anachronism was a fruitful one for fiction of the type of *The Naulakha*, which is more reminiscent of the romances of Kipling's friend Rider Haggard than of most of his own short fiction. At least one reviewer nevertheless saw the novel as in some sense true, remarking that 'several of the incidents can easily be capped by facts in Oriental history'.[42] The villain of the piece in *The Naulakha* may have reminded this reader of Zeenat Mahal, favourite wife of Bahadur Shah, the figurehead of the Mutiny. Grant says of her that 'With all the activity and zeal of an artful female intriguer, she set every secret engine to work to excite a hostile movement against the British Government' (p. 237). Like the imprisoned damsel, the wicked queen has her oriental counterpart.

The independent states of Central India, or Rajputana, were in fact popular both with Anglo-Indians and the wider British public because they enclosed the more 'primitive' and unique aspects of India on which they preferred to dwell, rather than the westernisation which they had set in motion. Here the irritations of bureaucratic government and the sordid elements in their own midst could be set aside. One might meet occasional white 'loafers' in search of dubious employment, but British troops and Eurasian clerks were left behind. Kipling has no contemporaries who write as caustically as himself on the machinery of government in British India, but there is plenty of evidence that he was not alone in his preference for remote and primitive places and people, as in this passage about Rajputana by the poet and historian Sir Alfred Lyall:

> The tract is mainly peopled by the aboriginal tribe of Bheels and the head man of a Bheel village is being examined touching a recent foray. A very black little man, with a wisp of cloth around his ragged loins, stands forth, bow and quiver in hand, swears by the dog, and speaks out sturdily: 'Here is the herd we lifted. We render back all but three cows, of which two we roasted and eat (sic) on the spot after harrying the village and the third we sold for a keg of liquor to wash down the flesh. As for the Brahman we shot in the scuffle, we will pay the proper blood money.' A slight shudder runs through the high-caste Hindu officials who record this candid statement; a sympathetic grin flits across the face of a huge Afghan, who has come wandering down for service or gang-robbery into these jungles where he is to the Bheels as a shark among small pike; and it is clear that we have got into a stratum of society far below Aryan or Brahmanic prejudices.[43]

Equally appealing was the court of a native rajah who still ruled with feudal ceremony. The last native ruler of major importance had been the Sikh chieftain Runjit Singh, of whom English readers might have read in Emily Eden's letters. The late nineteenth century, fascinated by the pomp of its own Queen's two jubilees, was probably more impressed by the wealth of a durbar (meeting) with Runjit than was Emily herself.

> Then we had a bale of shawls, and the Ayah got six shawls, and Mrs H a necklace, and, besides all the diamonds, they hung flowers all over us. We must have looked like mad, tragedy queens when we came out, but everybody was transmogrified in

the same way . . . there was G, sitting bolt upright, a pattern of patience, with a string of pearls as big as peas round his neck, a diamond ring on one hand and a large sapphire on the other, and a cocked hat embroidered in pearls at his side.[44]

Kipling toured these native states in his capacity as a journalist in 1887 and was much impressed. Bonamy Dobree speaks of the resulting 'delightful *Letters of Marque*, with their profound tolerance of India'; but this is tolerance, we must remember, for one favoured and atypical part of India.[45]

The Anglo-Indians, of whom Kipling was one, now deserve some separate consideration. They had a viewpoint of their own, and a special slang that still ('tiffin', a 'peg') seems to carry the musty, dusty flavour of the Raj with it. But England was still home, and few if any Englishmen actually chose to die in India. The customs of Anglo-India were those of England, somewhat altered, not to say petrified, by climate and circumstances generally. Conversely, the English ruling class saw no difficulty in transferring its accustomed way of life to India. Hunting, horse-racing and cricket, with the new addition of polo, were just as important in India; and so of course was the paying of calls, the giving of balls, and all the other elements of social life and entertainment. Holderness, significantly, thinks of the entire country in terms of a gentleman's country estate: 'The political boundaries of India have been laid out on a generous scale. It is as if the owner of a large estate in an unsettled country had taken in as much rough land as he thought was necessary for his privacy, and for keeping marauders off his fields and homestead.'[46] Thomas Huxley, espousing the Social Darwinism which was contributing to belief in the superiority of the white races, adds the garden to the house. Colonists, he says,

> set up a new Flora and Fauna and a new variety of mankind, within the old state of nature. Their farms and pastures represent a garden on a great scale, and themselves the gardeners who have to keep it up, in watchful antagonism to the old *régime*. Under the conditions supposed, there is no doubt of the result, if the work of the colonists be carried out energetically and with intelligent combination of all their forces.[47]

Anglo-India, for all the expansive metaphors, was undoubtedly a tightly-knit, inward-looking society. As Kipling himself said, it was a world in which 'every circumstance *and* relation of a man's life is public property.'[48] Even in comparison with other parts of the empire it can appear both stagnant and parochial, especially from the vantage point of the late twentieth century. One important factor in the atmosphere of the nineteenth century Raj that can be overlooked by a modern reader – it is not descernible in, for example, *A Passage to India* – is its strong military flavour. Anglo-India was torn between regarding itself as the natural ruling class, even as the inheritor of the Mughal Empire, and recognising its dependence on a relatively small army of occupation. It was a society further turned in on itself by effect of India's climate and vast physical distances on its small communities, and by the corresponding inquisitiveness of the people fortunate enough to gather in its hill stations.

Much of our sense of intimacy with this world is owed to Kipling. He certainly made the greatest contribution of all to the tradition that affirmed the self-sacrificing integrity of the Anglo-Indian civilian, and stressed how appalling were the conditions under which he lived. It depended, of course, whether one directed one's gaze towards the viceregal 'court' – the upper echelons of government and its hangers-on – whom Kipling himself appears ready to criticise, or to the lonely work of foresters, civil engineers and district officers in remote parts of the country. Crabbe's lines,

> But when returned the youth? The youth no more
> Returned exulting to his native shore;
> But in his stead there came a wornout man.

sum up the situation for Emily Eden, and her reminiscences would again be a likely source of information for Kipling's readers.

> The thing that chiefly interests me is to hear the details of the horrible solitude in which the poor young civilians live. Captain N. has led that sort of life in the jungles too, and says that, towards the end of the rainy season, when the health generally gives way, the lowness of spirits that comes on is quite dreadful, that every young man fancies he is going to die, and then thinks that nobody will bury him if he does, as there is no other European at hand.[49]

We must remember, however, that since Emily Eden's time the state of the country had changed considerably, particularly with the spread of the railways. *Kim* depicts a populous, cultivated country in which travel is well facilitated. Kipling himself tells us that he drew on the reminiscences of members of his club in Lahore, which is a reason for suspecting that some of his early work describes an era rather earlier than his own. In one respect Kipling's heroes differ from Miss Eden's Captain N. in that they are a special breed who are marked out for such work, like the Assistant Collector Gallio: ' "No-one wants my post", he used to say grimly, "and my Collector only pokes his nose in when he's quite certain that there is no fever. I'm monarch of all I survey!" '[50]

Undoubtedly there were some brave and intrepid Englishmen in India, cut off almost entirely from civilisation. But more to the point is the fact that all Anglo-Indians *felt* isolated. The Mutiny, as we have seen, had drawn them more tightly into their enclaves, and any threat to their position from administrators of liberal inclinations drew them together more tightly still. To preserve all the decorums of English society became a matter of ritual. No doubt they became attached to some of their servants, and their young children were entrusted to native servants and Eurasian governesses and often grew up fluent speakers of Hindi (Kipling and his sister had to be reminded as children to speak English in the drawing-room). It was nevertheless almost customary to affect comic despair at the incompetence or incomprehension of one's servants. It was to escape both such minor annoyances and the heat of the Indian summer that people came to Anglo-India's pleasure resort and summer capital, Simla. It was at Simla that the Viceroy conducted his government during the summer months when the climate in Calcutta was regarded as unbearable, and it was to Simla that Anglo-Indians who could afford it sent their wives and daughters from the heat of the Indian plains and where, inevitably, army officers on leave made their way in search of entertainment. It was situated in the Himalayan foothills, steep terrain to which the scented deodar forests, magnificent views, and the use of high-wheeled tongas, horses or litters as transport gave it a special, almost Alpine charm. There were other, similar hill-stations, like Mussoorie; but anyone who wanted to be anyone tried to get to Simla and its social whirl. It was in Simla that various rumours of scandal went the rounds, concerning the flirtations and suspected adulteries of wives who had left their husbands behind at their work, like the Jack Barrett of Kipling's grim ditty. What went on in Simla was probably exaggerated by gossip, but at the same time

Simla society offered a rare opportunity to frustrated individuals that was bound to be taken by some: for those with the means it was the safety-valve of an overly impersonal and duty-bound life. As a journalist Kipling was occasionally expected to describe Simla life, but also to be circumspect. It may have been as well for him that the Kipling family had gained the powerful friendship of the Viceroy, Lord Dufferin. At least one disgruntled Anglo-Indian thought him a 'cad', probably because of his professional work.[51] Even where Kipling does his best to involve the reader in his Simla stories the degree of boredom and inanity felt by all concerned that tends to come through reflects the mental privations of most white women in India. His most sympathetic and effective accounts of the tribulations of Anglo-Indian women, 'False Dawn' and 'A Wayside Comedy', are set in remote stations in the plains. Mrs Steel found outlets not only in writing, but in the kind of 'social work' that was becoming a pastime among some upper-class women in England; but to involve herself in this way with natives outside the household was an unusual course not open to every memsahib.

The popularity of these two themes, social gathering together and isolated working life, both rest on Anglo-India's perception of its unique position and collective expertise. The British in India naturally claimed that they knew how best to deal with Indians. They did not, however, claim that they knew a great deal about them. It was rather British aloofness and superiority, combined with open-handedness, that did the trick. While Kipling in an early story satirises the ignorance of the Viceroy's council by making an Anglo-Indian child who has talked to the servants responsible for getting an important piece of legislation changed, the more prevalent attitude is encapsulated in his biting contempt for the Russian spies in *Kim* who delude themselves into thinking that 'It is *we* who can deal with Orientals'.[52] Though Kipling has often been described as unusually knowledgeable about native life, his early work contains many warnings about the dangers of too much familiarity. Complementary to this attitude is an insistence on the inscrutability and unpredictability of all non-Europeans, incarnated in the thoroughly unprepossessing Amahagger tribe of H. Rider Haggard's popular novel *She* (1887). Kipling himself in an early poem turns the same supposed givens into an unsavoury recipe. Lord Dufferin says to his viceregal successor Lord Lansdowne:

You'll never plumb the Oriental mind,
And if you did it isn't worth the toil.
Think of a sleek French priest in Canada;
Divide by twenty half-breeds. Multiply
By twice the Sphinx's silence. There's your East,
And you're as wise as ever.

('One Viceroy Resigns')

Such attitudes were obviously open to criticism. The radical Francis Adams wrote the most trenchant early criticism of Kipling's work, remarking that in it Indians 'are to be viewed merely as a huge mass of raw, brown, naked humanity to be manipulated by the civil and military officials for the arcane purposes of the great Indian Empire'.[53] Adams' brief career, which ended in a trip to Alexandria to write against the British occupation, and where he committed suicide in 1893, seems almost symbolic of the defeat of the anti-imperialist lobby and its relegation to the fringes of the cultural milieu. For example, a short-lived journal called *The Butterfly* (1893) contains an article entitled 'Empire-Making (An Extract from the Child's Political Manual)' which satirises the 'blessings of gin and maxim guns' and the colonist's vocabulary of 'painful duty', 'sharp lesson' and 'protection'. Protection involves the continual expansion of territory in order to 'protect' the original possession, but Holderness, with no satirical intent, describes something very similar.

The Liberals under Gladstone were opposed in principle to maintaining the Empire, but they had failed to implement their policies in India in 1884, and had then lost face over Khartoum. At home Britain's loss of economic strength produced pressure to use the Empire's tame markets, and in 1886 Joseph Chamberlain split the party over the first Home Rule Bill for Ireland, and brought his Unionists into alliance with the Conservatives. He continued as a vigorous proponent of Empire, becoming Colonial Secretary in Lord Salisbury's administration and doing much to gain popular support. In truth the political struggle towards the end of the eighties was focused on the emergence of an organised working class at home, and critics of Empire were reduced to sniping at its cost, or to attacking moral standards. The Quaker Alfred Dyer exposed the lal bazaars of India, and Lord James Boyce turned the frequent comparison of Britain with imperial Rome against the imperialists; 'The government of India by England represents that of her provinces by Rome in being virtually despotic. In both cases, whatever may have been done for the people, nothing was or is done by the people,' – and so, incidentally, does one of the frayed citizens of Joyce's Dublin: 'The Roman, like the Englishman who follows in his footsteps, brought to every new shore on which he set his foot ... only his cloacal obsession.'[54]

Meanwhile, Kipling's reaction to liberals who accused the servants of Empire of being pampered or overpaid was vitriolic. The obvious target for his wrath was the Liberal 'Pagett, M. P.', one of the 'travelled idiots who duly misgovern the land'. To Kipling this visitor from Britain is a 'fluent liar' whose discomfiture he exults in. In this ditty the perspective is specifically Anglo-Indian, but Kipling soon learned to transform this championing of a particular group into an aggressive championing of the cause of Empire in lines like 'The English Flag', and this he did successfully, if sometimes controversially as well. His contempt for the 'Little Englanders' and the 'Pagetts' never diminished. In intellectual and literary circles generally Kipling had this field to himself. The Aesthetes were not concerned with such topics, William Morris was little read, and the work of Wells and Shaw was not yet known. At the same time, with the steady increase of contacts between India and the home country, Anglo-Indian views could already be heard sympathetically at home. *Punch* in 1890, for example, contains the following dialogue:

> 1st Distinguished Colonist: By the way, have you seen anything of that nice young fellow Lord Limpet, since you came to London. The man who stayed with you so many months at your station last year?
>
> 2nd Ditto Ditto: Oh yes. I met him the other night at Lady Burrill's reception and he kindly bestowed on me the unused half of a smile which he had put together for a passing Duke![55]

Simla apart, it was commonly believed that life in the colonies improved moral fibre. The mission of cultivating and civilising India was one that the British, though with large reservations as to its real advantages, regarded both as one that came naturally, and as a God-given duty. As Ruskin put it in his inaugural lecture at Oxford in 1870:

England must found colonies as far and fast as she is able, formed of her most energetic and worthiest men; seizing every piece of fruitful waste ground she can set her foot on, and there teaching these her colonies that their chief virtue is to be fidelity to their country, and their first aim is to be to advance the power of England by land and sea.[56]

Twenty years later public opinion, impressed by the recent annexation of Burma, felt that Ruskin's call was being answered. Wheeler's account of the taking of Burma from King Theebaw reflects the confident mood: 'In December Theebaw surrendered himself a prisoner and was deported to Madras . . . when the bandit leaders are rooted out, as they were rooted out of India in days gone by, Burma will become as prosperous as Bengal, whilst the river Irrawaddy will open a way towards China, and become more famous than the Ganges.' In 1889 Kipling concluded a newspaper article from Hong Kong by calling for the annexation of China.[57] British confidence also involved a supercilious rejection of France's less direct policy in the East, particularly with respect to its dealings with Theebaw, as another cartoon from *Punch* clearly shows (Plate 5). This portrayal by *Punch* of the British annexation of Burma genuinely reflects the general mood, limited as it always was by lack of information or intense interest, of a fair portion of the British reading public at the time. The animus of the cartoon and its bullying tone are features which not a few critics have also detected and deplored in Kipling's work. The braggadocio both of the cartoon and of Wheeler's dully complacent prose, reflect a confidence so aggressive as to suggest that beneath it lie some hidden anxieties. The solution is to simplify and standardise the notion of British superiority. Whatever the interest aroused by such remarkable figures as the eccentric Gordon or the entrepreneurial Rhodes, the brand of heroism offered for public consumption was bound up with a conformist racial identity, with 'Britishness' in the abstract, and stressed public-school 'initiative' rather than eccentricity. The stereotype wears regulation pith helmet, spurred boots, and takes upon himself, in the name of the Empress, a vigorous, prefect-style dispensation of 'justice'. Such an example scarcely contradicts the assertion that the Empire aroused little interest; public awareness at this level is a form of mental passivity. It is worth bearing in mind that such an attitude has not only sometimes been associated with Kipling, but has in the process fostered the misconception that it was Kipling who invented it. He did not, but the 'India' he projected for his readers is necessarily shaped by and set against the attitudes and emotions, ignorance included, that India and the Empire aroused. Alan Sandison gives an account of Kipling's personal vision, arguing that 'The individual self for Kipling was a precariously sustained artefact, and its integrity was necessarily the end of all one's calculations.'[58] Fear of anarchy is almost a trope of Kipling criticism, and for good reasons, but it does not directly answer the other critics who have rejected Kipling's work on the grounds that it offers little more than fantasy and wish-fulfilment. India itself can be regarded as a 'precariously sustained artefact', and to consider the kind of wish-fulfilment represented by the *Punch* cartoon is to understand the vehemence with which Kipling has sometimes been denounced. It is the more precise uses that Kipling made of his Indian theme, and how these affect his vision and his art, that remain to be explored.

In the sense that he was almost the first writer to use it as the subject of serious fiction, Kipling in some measure introduced India to the British public. For that public, however, India was a subject inevitably bound up with national identity and self-esteem. If one cannot merely summarise his fiction as messages of support for the Empire, neither can one treat it exactly as if Kipling's India was like Hardy's Wessex. India in all its aspects had long been public property, and the point was not so much to be responsive to it as to decide what to do with it next. Kipling introduced India into the literary world of the nineties, but what that culture understood by India would help in its turn to shape his style and vision.

2
Early Stages

Kipling's stories began to appear in England from 1888, when a thousand copies of the volume *Plain Tales from the Hills* were sent there from Calcutta by Thacker, Spink & Co. It was at the beginning of 1890, shortly after Kipling's own arrival, that his name really became known with the publication of *Soldiers Three* for the English market. The earliest stories in these volumes date back as far as 1884. In this chapter the early stages of Kipling's development as a writer of fiction are described. In the context of the British view of India outlined in Chapter 1 it is possible to see how Kipling's own approach to India assisted the transformation from Anglo-Indian journalist to the author who took London by storm in 1890.

For seven years, from the age of sixteen, Kipling lived, worked, and wrote in India. Short-sighted, unathletic, and already intensely 'literary', the schoolboy at the United Services College in Westward Ho! was clearly not destined, like many of his fellow pupils, for a career in the army. Instead, his parents found him a post as Assistant Editor on the *Civil and Military Gazette*. He was to be based in Lahore, capital of the Punjab, where his father was in charge of the museum described in the opening pages of *Kim*. Kipling must have had mixed feelings about this move, for while, as he stresses in his autobiography, it was a homecoming to his family and to India, is was also a decision in which he had no say. During the ten years that he was, like many Anglo-Indian children, boarded in England, he had spent many holidays at the home of his maternal uncle, the painter Edward Burne-Jones. The Grange in Fulham was a warm, friendly household, full of the comings and goings of the pre-Raphaelites and their friends. Kipling's recollections of it are either curtailed or marred by his later divergence in outlook from the generally liberal views of this side of his family, but their influence, combined with his romantic interest in a young art student named Violet Garrard and his desire to write poetry pointed towards a career in London. His parents had neither the means nor the wish to support such a career. It was to be delayed

31

until 1889, but in his 'Seven Years Hard' as an Anglo-Indian journalist Kipling laid its real foundations.

His life and its relation to his work have been thoroughly documented both in two full-length biographies and in a number of critical studies, and need not be summarised. Pertinent to this chapter, though, is the childhood memory with which he opened his elusive autobiography, aptly entitled *Something of Myself*: 'My first impression is of daybreak, light and colour and golden and purple fruits at the level of my shoulder . . . I have always felt the menacing darkness of tropical eventides, as I have loved the voices of night winds through palm or banana leaves, and the song of the tree-frogs.' Although there are, of course, dazzling descriptions of India throughout Kipling's fiction they do not, even in *Kim*, convey this sense of disinterested affection. The Bombay of his childhood exists for its own sake; to the Punjab of his young adulthood he owes an allegiance. In this chapter the development of Kipling's fiction will be examined in its early stages, between 1884 and 1889. During this period as a journalist in Anglo-India his writing took its particular shape not only as a result of his adjustment to the requirements of an Anglo-Indian audience, but as a result of his growing awareness of the political and cultural relationship between Britain and India.

Between the first and the last stories that he wrote in India Kipling travelled an enormous distance, both in mastering his craft as a writer and in discovering how he might exploit the circumstances in which he found himself. In 'The Gate of the Hundred Sorrows' (1884), the dominant note is helplessness. The author is content to record the monologue of an old Portuguese Eurasian drifting towards death in the confines of an opium den. In the last story written in India Kipling appears in his own person as a responsible, competent journalist. In this character he imposes due but triumphant proportion on the tale of 'The Man Who Would Be King', an allegory of Empire in which the epic, the tragic and the farcical are finely balanced. The contrast is suggestive both of the range of dramatic possibilities that Kipling was able to discover in the short story and of his need for a secure identity from which to launch them.

Louis Cornell has traced a line of development from Kipling's schoolboy verse – 'Schoolboy Lyrics' and 'Sundry Phansies' to 'The Gate of the Hundred Sorrows'. The story takes its dreamlike atmosphere from a schoolboy poem entitled 'Paul Vaugel', though it also shows already a sharp eye for the social customs of the underworld it describes. The verse that Kipling actually published in India (his mother had issued 'Schoolboy Lyrics' without his permission) is in the completely different idiom of Anglo-Indian light humour; a communal rhetoric which is the basis of his later ballads and public poems. There is a similar though less obvious dichotomy in his early prose, and again research has enabled a distinction to be drawn between stories that represent an attempt to escape from journalism into literature and those that build on the experience that he was gaining as a journalist.[1] Important as this change is, it is equally important not to overstate it. Early monologes like 'The Gate of the Hundred Sorrows' and 'The Dream of Duncan Parrenness' are indeed self-conscious literary exercises for which a remote and circumscribed aspect of India is the excuse, but this does not mean that the impact of India on the young journalist's senses spontaneously generates a new and more robust style. On the one hand India's impact was not confined to his senses – he was also confronted with the dilemmas of British rule; on the other there is nothing spontaneous about the way his grasp of literary forms was brought to bear on the subjects he encountered as a reporter.

Another early monologue, 'The Strange Ride of Morrowbie Jukes', clearly shows Kipling setting out to find ways of making literature from the preoccupations of Anglo-India. Morrowbie Jukes is a civil engineer, of a precise and unimaginative disposition, who tumbles into a sand ravine where Hindus who have revived on the funeral pyre have been cast into earthly limbo. These unfortunates live in greasy burrows and eat crows, from which Jukes's horse makes a welcome change in diet. In this situation Jukes's authority as a white sahib is meaningless. He has to preserve what cleanliness and decorum he can, and guard his back until he is rescued. The story is a fable about Anglo-Indian fears of a 'republic' in which black and white meet on equal terms, and of the insidious pressure they felt at the mere presence of their Hindu subjects. As Suzanne Howe says in her *Novels of Empire*, 'Compared to the relatively sunny and daylight problems of high and dry Africa and Australia, everything in India was alien, mysterious, hostile, in a thousand complex, "unfair" ways. Nothing was out in the open.'[2] The atmosphere that Kipling creates in this story is strikingly reminiscent of Poe, and like Poe's 'The Facts in the Case of M. Valdemar', this story could easily be mistaken for a factual account.[3] In the Poe story, however, we accompany the narrator half unwillingly, questioning the rightness of allowing oneself to be implicated in such ghastly events. In Kipling's story there is no such dilemma. 'Morrowbie Jukes' captures one dimension of Anglo-Indian life, but the horror story is used simply to equate India with ghastliness.

In 1886 Kipling's rather dour editor on the *Civil and Military Gazette*, Stephen Wheeler, was replaced by a younger man. E. Kay Robinson had been instructed to put some sparkle into the paper, and under his direction Kipling began to write 'turnovers' – stories of 1500 to 2000 words that began on the first page and continued overleaf. It was these stories that formed the basis of the volume *Plain Tales from the Hills*. All the Anglo-Indian papers of the time published a good deal of poetry; verse on Anglo-Indian themes, like the collection of *Departmental Ditties* that brought Kipling his first success. His 'turnovers' could thus be sure of a fair reception, but Kipling and Robinson's project was still a lively and ambitious one. In a community that obviously could not sustain literary journals like the *English Illustrated Magazine* or *Blackwood's*, they were seeking to inject something of the same aura into a provincial 'rag'. That Anglo-India was ripe for such an initiative is demonstrated by Kipling's progress onto the *Pioneer* at Allahabad, where he was able to write stories of up to 5000 words, and by the collection of his work in Thacker, Spink and Co's 'Indian Railway Library' series. Writing to satisfy demand, Kipling had to present his audience with an image of their 'India'. Some of the results were understandably trivial, but it was a process that impelled him to explore and experiment with his subject.

One striking feature of the 'turnovers' is the compression and incisiveness with which a specifically 'Indian' situation is set up:

> Fate and the Government of India have turned the Station of Kashima into a prison.
>
> ('A Wayside Comedy')

> Well, she was a *very* sweet girl and very pious, but for many reasons she was impossible.... The little opal-tinted onyx at the base of her fingernails said this as plainly as print.
>
> ('Kidnapped' – of a Eurasian girl)

> In India, where you really see humanity – raw, brown, naked humanity – with nothing between it and the blazing sky, and

only the used-up, over-handled earth underfoot, the notion somehow dies away, and most folk come back to simpler theories.

('The Conversion of Aurelian McGoggin')

A man should, whatever happens, keep to his own caste, race, and breed. Let the White go to the White and the Black to the Black. Then, whatever trouble falls is in the ordinary course of things – neither sudden, alien, nor unexpected.

('Beyond the Pale')

Following a suggestion of Randall Jarrell's, Cornell describes these stories as 'moral experiments'.[4] Taken in the sense that Kipling manages in these miniatures to allow a degree of ambiguity in the make up of his characters this is an implausible notion. Mulvaney is one of the most colourful and complex of Kipling's characters, but his drunkenness and (carefully restricted) sexual latitude do not really challenge expectation. He is not subjected to the blatant hero-worship that Kipling lavishes on Bobby Wick in 'Only a Subaltern', but he is perfectly adequate to his role in the social hierarchy, and his weaknesses are indeed a kind of caste-mark. More than that, his faults even assist the training of the army in India, as he explains in 'The Courting of Dinah Shadd':

> I'm fit only to tache the new drafts what I'll niver learn myself; an' I am sure, as tho' I heard ut, that the minut wan av these pink-eyed recruities gets away from my 'Mind ye now', an' 'Listen to this, Jim, bhoy', – sure I am that the sergint houlds me up to him for a warnin'. So I tache, as they say at musketry instructions, by direct and ricochet fire.

In another sense, however, 'moral experiment' has a certain aptness, for Kipling's fiction was probing the social life of Anglo-India to unprecendented depths; disturbing its politer strata at times, but also making more concrete the mingled feelings of duty and disdain to which native India was treated. In a related but broader sense it also suggests the quality that Kipling's stories have of balancing themselves between the 'new' writing of the period and the literary establishment. His idiom is modern and experimental in its compression and vividness, and its use of slang and dialect, but the tone retains the conventional moral undertow of Victorian fiction. In 'A Wayside Comedy', for example, the grim little tale of adultery allows sympathy to be allotted to the different characters along entirely conventional lines, with the original philanderer easily coming off worst. The innocent Mrs Vansuythen is 'a fair woman, with very still grey eyes, the colour of a lake just before the sun touches it. No man who had seen those eyes could, later on, explain what fashion of woman she was to look upon.' The bald statement later on that she was 'only an ordinarily good woman' does not remedy an emphasis that is not at all in the spirit of De Maupassant, whose influence is perhaps detectable in the theme and in the cool detachment of the narrator. Kipling's vision of torment arises not from the native hypocrisy of the characters but from their imprisonment in their Station, and the story is written on behalf of the isolated European communities in India.

To write within the assumptions and values of his Anglo-Indian readers affords Kipling the opportunity to use a natural economy of means, as in the use of the 'prison' motif in 'A Wayside Comedy' The sense of isolation and confinement can be sustained by the mere mention of the 'rock-tipped circle of the Dosehri hills' and the 'long white line of the Narkarra road', and the complete absence of Indians from the story which reinforces this sense of emptiness is perfectly acceptable. The expansive view of India as the Englishman's country estate obviously conflicts with this scene-setting, but it belongs to another group of ideas. Such different sets of assumptions in the end overlap and reinforce one another. The isolation in 'A Wayside Comedy' is possible because when Indians do appear in Anglo-Indian literature they are uncivilised and rarely capable of social intercourse, and when attention is directed to the question of British 'ownership' of India its people are regarded as no more than the local fauna. To this Anglo-Indian perspective Kipling brought his taut and colourful sentences, designed to make the 'India' under scrutiny expand like a paper flower. A brilliant and very early example is 'The Story of Muhammed Din', in which the casual but delicately systematic observation of the small boy seems to echo the tone of Gilbert White's *Natural History of Selborne*. Here Kipling has an extra ace up his sleeve when the doctor who attends Muhammed Din shatters the 'naturalist's' gentle perspective with the comment, 'They have no stamina, these brats'. That life in India is cheap is another trope; but closely as Kipling identified himself with Anglo-Indian society, he was also capable of a certain amount of criticism and satire, particularly in his view of Simla. With Mrs Hauksbee, who also appears in a number of stories, the flatness of the character is evidently functional. There is a subtle irony in the callow young narrator's admiration for her, as it begins to dawn on the reader that it is the shallowness of Simla society that affords her her position and her pretensions to a 'salon'. Although Mrs Hauksbee had an original whom Kipling undoubtedly did admire, there is a deeper awareness that almost any woman, given the circumstances, could play at being 'The Wittiest Woman in India'. 'The Story of the Gadsbys', which Kipling described as 'an Anglo-Indian autour de mariage' has more serious intentions, but the degree of emotional involvement is balanced by sardonic touches. The series of dialogues contains one striking exercise in Dickensian sentiment when the young wife is at death's door, while the whole work seems to be inspired by the 'theatricals' in which Kipling sometimes took part. When we learn that Gadsby's mistress, Harriet Herriot, is 'like a name in a novel', or when the gallant soldier turns 'the colour of good cigar ash', we must suspect that Kipling is also amusing himself at the expense of these amateur productions.

The chief demerit of Kipling's early style, as many critics have pointed out, is the obtrusiveness of a narrator who has a constant air of being 'in the know'. Philip Mason is surely right in attributing this attitude to Kipling's need to identify himself with his community, and more especially when he was writing about the 'native' underworld, with which respectable people had no contact.[5] He was in a particularly vulnerable position both as a very young man in a world where seniority was important, and as a mere journalist, commenting on rather than fulfilling the imperatives of the Raj. The narrator who warns that 'A man should, whatever happens, keep to his own caste, race and breed' is very clearly claiming a measure of self-protection in 'Beyond the Pale'. There is, however, no easy line to be drawn between the young author's protecting himself from his readers and protecting himself from himself. Certain topics might require careful handling not only to safeguard the author's reputation, but in order not to expose any contradictions in the conception of India he puts forward. A plain example of the narrator being used simply to keep a safe distance occurs in 'The Phantom Rickshaw'. Originally this story was a simple monologue, but when it was republished Kipling rewrote it in order to lighten the effect of Jack Pansay's sordid recollections: 'When he recovered I suggested that he should write out the whole affair from beginning to end, knowing that ink might assist him to ease his mind. He was in a high fever while he was writing, and the blood-and-thunder magazine diction he adopted did not calm him.' Whether or not the actual Kipling persona is present, the narration is often forceful as well as vivid, and sometimes intrusively so; but this effect is a necessary consequence of the short pieces he was writing in more ways than one. As we have seen, the British both in India and at home had a growing sense of the Raj as part of a purposeful and coherent project. Kipling's diverse and sharply observant Indian contes had at least to avoid detracting from this need for coherence; but his style of writing suggests literary allegiances that were in some ways at odds with the cohesive spirit of imperialism.

The mid-Victorian years of economic prosperity had also been the years in which the novel reached its greatest heights. These novelists – Dickens, Mrs Gaskell, Thackeray, George Eliot, had to a greater or lesser degree a capacity to create an entire social world of individuals working out their destinies in concert. Disraeli in *Sybil, or the Two Nations* could employ the same broad canvas in a plea for social and political unity. In the succeeding decades that confidence in ultimate social harmony had given way to a more sceptical mood. Contributing to this feeling were the influence of Darwin's theory of evolution and the corresponding loss of certainty in religion, and the progress of the industrial revolution, rendering the aristocracy – the traditional preservers of culture – more and more obsolete, and raising the spectre of a takeover by the uneducated masses – the 'Demos' of Gissing's novel. While Hardy and Gissing were, in quite different ways, writing novels that were less than sanguine about the worlds they depicted, the Aesthetic movement had discovered its publicist in Oscar Wilde, and was about to become 'Decadent'. It held to an assurance of art's superiority over life and its indifference to morality that was unnerving to those who did not lay claim to the artistic temperament. If the movement was considered morally suspect and overly pretentious in British society, its contempt for practical endeavours was totally antipathetic to the Anglo-Indian world. Kipling soon found that he had no time either for what he considered the political naiveties of his former 'Uncle Topsy', William Morris, or for the studied indifference of Oscar Wilde. Yet he could not avoid the new emphasis on the importance of art in general, or the wider note of weariness and constraint of which the flamboyant aesthetic pose was only one expression. One of his grimmest accounts of the Indian hot weather in 'At the End of the Passage' begins

Four men, each entitled to 'life, liberty, and the pursuit of happiness', sat at a table playing whist. The thermometer marked – for them – one hundred and one degrees of heat. The room was darkened till it was only just possible to distinguish the pips of the cards and the very white faces of the players. A tattered, rotten punkah of whitewashed calico was puddling the hot air and whining dolefully at each stroke. Outside lay the gloom of a November day in London.

The physical sufferings of the men at this card party, where the darkness of the room is a necessity, is in satiric contrast to the studied boredom of the young men of Wilde or George Moore, surrounded by the comforts of a London which is not just a heat mirage. Against fashionable scepticism he affirms a stoical conception of duty, but in turning the tables in this way Kipling naturally shares much of the aesthetic or decadent structure of feeling. Life is no longer part of a predestined harmony but a partial struggle that has to be represented in a partial, impressionistic way. Kipling's characters stand out against their unfamiliar surroundings with an immediacy that gives the impression, as Wilde himself said admiringly, of 'reading life by superb flashes of vulgarity'.[6] The lines prefacing 'At the End of the Passage', which describe the 'soul of man' being blown like dust from a thoroughly despondent body also echo the decadent mood, as does the vague 'horror' with which it ends.

'At the End of the Passage' was one of the stories written in 1890, during Kipling's first astonishingly successful year in London. It has been said that the Aesthetes rebuffed him, but dislike was strong on Kipling's side. Almost as soon as he arrived in London he derided the artists in 'velvet collar-rolls' who 'moo and coo about their blessed souls'. They were lampooned with serious intent in his poem about the bookish 'Tomlinson', who turns out to have no soul of his own because he has refined it out of existence in his quest for 'sensibility'.[7] Kipling believed in his own 'daemon' of inspiration that was with him in his best work, but he abhorred the self-conscious attitude towards art. 'Wait, drift, obey' was his own writer's motto. In London he had a new platform and a new context in which to place his experience of India, and he soon discovered his ability to appeal to the less aesthetically inclined of his new audience. Wilde's comment had had its sequel when a number of Anglo-Indians complained that Wilde had called them vulgar.

Wilde airily replied that the world depicted by Kipling was vulgar, but that he had no interest in, much less knowledge of, its correspondence with reality.[8] However, Kipling's championing of the manly, imperial virtues had caught on, and for that reason it had to be assumed that his stories *did* mirror Anglo-Indian society. His work was henceforth to be regarded as realistic in a way that imposed on him a responsibility for its moral tone. Stories like 'A Wayside Comedy', quite unexceptionable as a treatment of a common Anglo-Indian theme (one new novel of 1888, for example, bore the title *A Moral Bigamist: a Story of Ourselves in India*), now came under fire through the accident of their republication in England during the vogue for a more sonorous, serious Kipling.[9] The moral guardians of the *Edinburgh Review* and the *Quarterly Review* took exception to Kipling's phrase about certain of his Anglo-Indian characters 'playing tennis with the seventh comandment'. They did not share Wilde's lightheartedness towards the Raj, and quickly warned Kipling not to share it either. They need not have worried.[10]

At about this time, under the impact of looking at India from the vantage point of London, Kipling himself began to think of his work as a serious project. As he remembered in *Something of Myself* (4), 'my original notion grew into a vast, vague conspectus – Army and Navy Stores List if you like – of the whole sweep and meaning of things and effort and origins throughout the Empire. I visualised it . . . in the shape of a semi-circle of buildings and temples projecting into a sea – of dreams.' The difficulty was to realise this project in the face of a privileging of the particular moment over the coherent whole that went deeper than political and artistic differences. Kipling could ask 'What do they know of England that only England know?', or blatantly assert that 'God has arranged that a clean-run youth of the British middle classes shall, in the matter of backbone, brains, and bowels, surpass all other youths.'[11] He could also produce lifelike miniatures that prompted comparison with the French travel writer Pierre Loti. To unite sentiment and description successfully, and prove his vision of Empire on recalcitrant British pulses was a more difficult undertaking. 'The Head of the District', which first appeared in *Macmillan's Magazine* for January 1890 is one of Kipling's more notorious, and perhaps least read stories, because of its blunt political satire on the 'principles of Liberal government', but it nevertheless represents a serious attempt to bring this vision to life.

The story tells of the consequences of the appointment of an

Oxford-educated Bengali civil servant to a frontier district peopled by a tribe who traditionally despise his race.

> Bengalis were as scarce as poodles among the simple borderers, who cut each other's heads open with long spades and worshipped impartially at Hindu and Mohammedan shrines. They crowded to see him, pointing at him, and diversely comparing him to a gravid milch-buffalo, or a broken-down horse, as their limited range of metaphor prompted. They laughed at his police guard, and wished to know how long the burly Sikhs were going to lead Bengali apes. They enquired whether he had brought his women with him, and advised him explicitly not to tamper with theirs.

The style here is clearly that of the journalist at his relaxed best; detached, knowledgeable, and ready with a mordant simile. The lightly satirical tone, the trademark of the shorter *Plain Tales*, is adequate to despatch the unfortunate Grish Chunder De, the educated 'babu'. But Kipling here wants to imbue the story of De's appointment and ignominious departure at the first sign of rebellion with the 'whole sweep and meaning of things', and to that end he constructs the story out of a number of other devices.

It opens on a note of pathos and portent, as the previous district officer dies while watching the sail of his wife's boat tacking and blundering up and down the swollen river. Clearly the times are out of joint, and the sail foreshadows the consequences of De's appointment. After this the sneering portrait of the Viceroy who appoints De is simply otiose, and only serves to remind us that Kipling had been humiliated at the Punjab club when his newspaper had supported the abortive Ilbert Bill in 1884. The effeminate Bengali is counterpointed by the blind mullah who incites the revolt, for with his barbed tongue and physical deformities this figure is more like the wicked witch than the conventional Pathan. On the opposite side are the two 'strong men', the warrior Khoda Dad Khan, and the deputy in the district, Tallantire. when the revolt fails Khoda Dad Khan succeeds the mullah, whose murder is described with the same anthropological detachment as the arrival of Grish Chunder De. When we turn to the actions of the white men, however, the reporter suddenly adopts a more full-blooded romantic tone. The terse, economical style collapses in a flood of adjectives as 'Tallantire drove his spurs into a rampant skewbald stallion with china blue eyes, and settled himself for the forty-mile ride to fort Ziar'; and his success is crowned with this familiar image: 'By sundown began the remorseless patrol of the border by police and trooper, most like the cow-boys' eternal ride round restless cattle.'

The truth-to-life of 'The Head of the District' was much praised by its early reviewers. To some extent one can discount the opinions of those who approved of Kipling's polemic, but a little more is needed to explain the way in which the fairly obvious manipulation of the reader was overlooked. The effect of the story depends very largely on acceptance of the proposition that *all* natives, both the Khursu Kheyl and the Bengali, are fundamentally different; notably in their fecklessness and irresponsibility. The British, as the story repeatedly emphasises, will stay at their posts even in the most adverse conditions. If this is taken for granted then the overpowering *manhood* of the British becomes correspondingly easier to swallow. In this respect the loyalty and resourcefulness of Khoda Dad Khan actually pose something of a problem. The scene of the mullah's death, however, emphasises the savage side to his character, and to make more sure, he enters at the end of the story with the severed head of De's brother.

> 'Who art thou, seller of dog's flesh', thundered Tallantire, 'to speak of terms and treaties? Get hence to the hills – go, and wait there starving, till it shall please the Government to call thy people out for punishment – children and fools that ye be! Count your dead and be still. Rest assured that the Government will send you a man!' 'Ay', returned Khoda Dad Khan, 'for we also be men.' As he looked at Tallantire between the eyes, he added, 'And by God, Sahib, mayest thou be that man!'

Thus the two governing ideas of the story, of the natives being 'children' and of the need for a proper man in charge, are fused in the conclusion.

'The Head of the District' is a piece of special pleading, and one that is marred by some exceptionally clumsy sarcasm, but it is also true that Kipling has worked out his theme in detail. To say, as Suzanne Howe does, that 'his bouncing virtuosity, his gentlemanly, sporting stress on The Game and The Law, his evocations of thick Indian atmosphere, form a kind of screen for the fact that his view of India was limited, sheltered and slick' is to underestimate him.[12] In this story Kipling adopts much from popular romance, but he is also, within the limits of his right-wing bias, examining some of the implications of British rule. Grish Chunder De and Khoda Dad Khan are characters in a way that the amorphous savage or clown of much popular literature set in India was not. Even the picture of two native clerks falling asleep on the pile of telegrams despatched by the frantic Grish Chunder De, malicious though it is, contributes to an impression of carefully observed detail. A careful balance has also been struck between affection for and aversion from the Khursu Kheyl, which might easily have been avoided by reducing them to anonymous savages. It is precisely because Kipling is willing to deal with India in such concrete terms that he adopts a narrative style that is sometimes forceful and brusque. It is exemplified by the forcing together of key ideas at the end of 'The Head of the District', but there is a difference between this forcefulness and mere slickness. Kipling's view is that of British Imperialism in a state of rare alertness and attention to detail and the story does convey the state of tension inherent not only in the particular situation, but in the British experience of governing India. The overt control that Kipling exercises over the elements of the story is an indication not only of his need to maintain Anglo-Indian respectability for himself, but of the attempt to work his vivid impressions of India into a statement of the white man's role.

Many writers on Kipling have stressed his unusually detailed knowledge of the life of Indians, based on his own brief account in *Something of Myself* (3):

> I would wander till dawn in all manner of odd places – liquor shops, gambling and opium dens, which are not a bit mysterious, wayside entertainments such as puppet shows, native dances; or in and about the narrow gullies under the mosque of Wazir Khan. . . . One would come home, just as the light broke, in some night-hawk of a hired carriage which stank of hookah-fumes, jasmine-flowers and sandalwood; and if the driver were moved to talk, he told one a good deal.

It has been pointed out that he knew correspondingly little of the educated Indians of the middle-class, but here the widespread contempt for 'babus' is more significant than actual knowledge. The importance of Kipling's personal experiences is particularly hard to assess because he is really the only Anglo-Indian writer who not only describes in detail the colourful and sensuous life of India but also brings into play the popular notions of India as a darkly seductive but also terrifying place. In one respect this may seem an odd thing to say, since the majority of his tales are not set in the tropical Southern India of the popular imagination but in the northern plains – the Punjab where he lived and worked. (It will be interesting, in a later chapter, to note the use that Kipling makes in the *Jungle Books* of the Seonee jungle which he never visited in person.) However, he has no difficulty in evoking the kind of thickly-textured scene that combines the elements of Oriental danger and desire for his readers.

In 'Beyond the Pale', Bisesa's room 'looked out through the grated window into the narrow dark gully where the sun never came and where the buffaloes wallowed in the blue slime.' The sexual metaphor of the gully and the grating through which the Englishman, Trejago, gains access to Bisesa is rather too heavily embossed, but it forms part of a world of exotic objects like the coded message consisting of 'the half of a broken glass-bangle, one flower of the blood-red dhak, a pinch of *bhusa* or cattle-food, and eleven cardamoms' that is, in its own way, in the 'aesthetic' mould, and astonishingly so for 1884. 'Beyond the Pale' is surely the most remarkable of the 'Plain Tales' for the vivid sense of sympathetic involvement in the forbidden love-affair that it encourages: 'Trejago laughed, and Bisesa stamped her feet – little feet, light as marigold flowers, that could lie in the palm of a man's one hand.' Equally remarkable, though, is the energy with which these emotions are put into their social perspective. Louis Cornell has suggested that the narrator's strict warning that a man should keep to his own caste, race, and creed is there to be undermined, but the parallel that he sees with Abelard and Heloise is scarcely consistent with Trejago's return to everyday life at the end.[13] At the most intimate moments the narrative, as with the marigolds, hints at inevitable impermanence, and however much we pity Bisesa she is less an individual than, in the catch-all phrase, a 'child'. Her dreadful mutilation is used to reinforce Trejago's symbolic state of castration (he is also wounded in the groin), after which he is unable to penetrate the mysterious alleyways of the East again. The illicit nature of the love affair finally isolates it so completely that Trejago can return to his everyday life, where he is reckoned 'a very decent sort of man'. 'Love heeds not caste, not sleep a broken bed. I went in search of love and lost myself' declares the heading to 'Beyond the Pale'; but Trejago goes in search of love without, in the end, risking his white identity. In one of the earliest reviews of Kipling's work Andrew Lang singled out the elliptical, incomplete quality that gives the story its romantic charm; but it is as a social document and a warning that 'Beyond the Pale' is really completed: 'He has lost her in the City where each man's house is guarded and unknowable as the grave; and the grating that opens into Amir Nath's gully has been walled up.'

Plain Tales from the Hills was reviewed as a book for a male readership, for as Andrew Lang put it, 'The "average" novel-reader, who likes her three stout volumes full of the love affairs of an ordinary young lady in ordinary circumstances will not care for Mr Kipling's brief and lively stories.'[14] Such early reviews identify the consumers of *Plain Tales* and 'The Gadsbys' as the 'smoking-room' set; that is, the semi-adolescent market for which James Bond and *The Virgin Soldiers* caters in the twentieth century. It is worth noting, though, how different 'Beyond the Pale' really is from most such fiction. While it combines the usual elements of dangerous adventure and sex-interest, Trejago's failure and implicit castration are scarcely the comfortable wish-fulfilment that we expect of the genre as a whole. This is not to say that Kipling was deliberately writing within what we now recognise as a genre of sorts. In his period, while sex was not, of course, described so explicitly, the Orient was, as we have seen, *the* sphere in which sexual freedom was covertly expected. To deal with the situation described in 'Beyond the Pale' was thus to be writing for the 'smoking-room' whether one liked it or not.

As we shall see when we look at the range of journals to which he contributed, there can be little doubt that Kipling knew how to make his stories marketable. But his desire to chronicle and illuminate the Empire was never far away. The tension between the detachment appropriate to rulers and the need for a close understanding of India is doubled by the tension between attraction to and repulsion from this India; by the mixture of fear and desire with which it was generally met, whether this takes the form of explicit sexual adventure or not. In a very early story like 'Beyond the Pale' the sensual impact of the Indian scene is simply weighed against the resolute detachment of the narrator, but the history of Kipling's early development is of his growing ability not merely to respond to the tension inherent in such situations but to rearrange it. Whereas many of the stories in *Plain Tales* may strike us as incidents that Kipling had come across and had then 'jazzed up' a little, some of the longer stories in the Indian Railway Library volumes and in *Life's Handicap* attempt to create fictional worlds in which the characters learn and suffer. 'The Courting of Dinah Shadd', 'On Greenhow Hill', and 'Without Benefit of Clergy' are among the most striking and well-known examples.

The brevity of Kipling's turnovers imposes obvious limitations on them, and these are sometimes compounded by the clannish perspective of the Anglo-Indian. The dust-storm in another Plain Tale, 'False Dawn', ought to represent well the power of India to darken the mind of the European, but there is little enough to darken in the flat, unsympathetic characters. The final scene in which the dust-covered assembly of Anglo-Indians applaud the newly-engaged couple – and themselves for having managed to preserve decorum – is the theatrical moment for which the preceding tale seems to be little more than the excuse. 'I never knew anything so un-English in my life' comments the narrator, with a nicely-judged irony at least. Such judgement is completely lacking in 'Kidnapped', although part of the problem is that in this tale Kipling uses a convention that we no longer recognise. Here a promising young Civilian gets engaged to a Eurasian girl, but is 'saved' when his friends forcibly detain him on the wedding day. The social code which insists that there is nothing wrong with this brutal interference, but which damns the prospective father-in-law because 'He said things – vulgar and impossible things which showed the raw, rough "ranker" below the "Honorary", and I fancy Peythroppe's eyes were opened', is one that we are not inclined to accept. 'Practical joking' of this kind was to get Kipling into trouble with the critics in *Stalky & Co.*, which is set in a public school, but in which the young heroes frequently impress us as adult in outlook and resources; 'like hideous little men', as Robert Buchanan put it. H. G. Wells saw in *Stalky* 'the key to the ugliest, most retrogressive, and finally fatal idea of modern imperialism; the idea of a tacit conspiracy between the law and illegal violence.'[15]

The common occurrence of such incidents in many of Kipling's humorous stories derives in part from their acceptability in the Anglo-Indian ethos, and 'Kidnapped' is an example of the way they percolated from the militarism of the political Raj into everyday life. The easy resort to violence as a necessary means of maintaining order is not only a general feature of the ruling-class British attitude towards its colonies, and indeed towards its own working-class, as the Trafalgar Square demonstration of 1888 and the violent suppression of strikes in the early nineties clearly show – it can also act, in daily life, as a kind of 'purgative' for the erotic, unmanning aspect of India. Kipling sometimes describes this with some understanding and power in his soldier stories. The problem with 'Kidnapped' is that this eroticism is nowhere felt in the story, and the conspiracy to stop the marriage thus lacks even the 'gut-reaction' type of justification. The commonplace connection between India and female sexuality was bound to be important to Kipling as he sought to combine attraction with repulsion, stewardship with involvement, fiction for a self-consciously moral reading public with sensuous brevity. His use of it requires careful consideration.

His own voyeurism has been criticised. Martin Fido, for example, thinks that, probably because of his unhappy teenage love affair with Violet Garrard, 'he veered horribly between the sickly sentiment of an overgrown calf-love, and its concomitant romanticising of the erotic'[16] The attitude being castigated was, in many ways, part of the period. What may be true is that the combination of Kipling's subject with his attempt to write in a 'new' way make the attitude stand out in his work. As Andrew Lang had pointed out, serious Anglo-Indian fiction of any kind was a rare commodity. The novels of Marion Crawford and Mrs Steel blandly ignore the conception of India as female that is so evident in the popular press. For Kipling, by contrast, whether he romanticised it or not, eroticism was basic to his sense of India, and it is present in his journalism as well as in his fiction.

In November and December of 1887 he made a tour for his newspaper of the independent native states of Central India. The articles that he wrote for the *Pioneer* were published under the title *Letters of Marque* and later collected in *From Sea to Sea*. Kipling naturally reports his conversations with the white men in these remote, often semi-desert regions – the political representatives, and the travelling salesmen and contractors. He makes the expected contrast between the excellence of the hospitals, canals and museums that an enlightened Rajah can afford, and those of British India. He visits the historical monuments, takes part in a shoot, and visits a royal stables. But it is his indirect encounters with women that act as a touchstone for the quality of the experiences that he finds in different places.

The journey begins, inevitably, with the Taj Mahal, and equally inevitably, perhaps, a trope about femininity crosses Kipling's mind:

> To the one who watched and wondered that November morning the thing seemed full of sorrow – the sorrow of the man who built it for the woman he loved, and the sorrow of the workmen who died in the building – used up like cattle. And in the face of this sorrow the Taj flushed in the sunlight and was beautiful, after the beauty of a woman who has done no wrong. (I)

In the friendly state of Udaipur he enjoys the colourful display of the women bathing, 'clad in raw vermilion, dull red, indigo and sky blue, saffron and pink and turquoise'. At the end of his description, however, the scene takes on a magnetic sensuality: 'Then a woman rose up, and clasping her hands behind her head, looked at the passing boat, and the ripples spread out from her waist, in blinding white silver, far across the water.' It is indeed a somewhat callow and voyeuristic Kipling who spoils the effect here by adding, 'As a picture, a daringly insolent picture, it was superb.' (VII) The mood is darker in the derelict ancient city of Chitor, a setting that struck him strongly enough to be used in *The Naulakha*.

> The Englishman slipped and bumped on the rocks, and arrived, more suddenly than he desired, upon the edge of a dull blue tank, sunk between walls of timeless masonry. In a slabbed-in recess, water was pouring through a shapeless stone gargoyle, into a trough; which trough again dripped into the tank. Almost under the little trickle of water, was the loathsome Emblem of Creation, and there were flowers and rice around it . . . It seemed as though the descent had led the Englishman, firstly, two thousand years from his own century, and secondly, into a trap, and that he would fall off the polished stones into the stinking tank, or that the Gau Mukh would continue to pour water until the tank rose up and swamped him, or that some of the stone slabs would fall forward and crush him flat. Then he was conscious of remembering, with peculiar and unnecessary distinctness, that, from the Gau Mukh, a passage let to the subterranean chambers in which the fair Pudmini and her handmaidens had slain themselves. (XI)

As with Amir Nath's gully in 'Beyond the Pale', Kipling turns the locale into a somewhat overpowering sexual metaphor, save that here desire is overwhelmed by fear. The description of the tank is used to express a morbid horror of the female sexual organ, which is perceived, picking out the adjectives Kipling employs, as a swampy, stinking, loathsome, shapeless, timeless trap. The white male's fear of the ancient, subterranean India that lay beneath the skeins of his civilisation is never more clearly exposed. Boondi, the last place that Kipling visits, is also the most remote and the most hostile. Women are kept out of sight, but almost inevitably he hears in the palace 'a woman's voice singing, and the voice rang as do voices in caves.'

It would not be hard to guess that this journalist is writing for a predominantly masculine society in these articles, but although the latent sexual feelings expressed are common to Orientalists, they are used with less than the usual arrogance and detachment. Observant and delighted as the young journalist sometimes is, he is also nervous and afraid of the dark. Ironically, his name for himself, 'the Englishman', which should be synonymous with confidence and phlegm, comes to subtly accentuate an underlying isolation and vulnerability.

Kipling's prolonged adolescent phase emerges clearly from a passage in the second part of *From Sea to Sea*, describing the stockyards of Chicago that he visited two years later on his way from India to London:

> Women come sometimes to see the slaughter, as they would come to see the slaughter of men. And there entered that vermilion hall a young woman of large mould, with brilliantly scarlet lips, and heavy eyebrows, and hair that came down in a 'widow's peak' on her forehead. She was well and healthy and alive, and she was dressed in flaming red and black, and her feet . . . were cased in red leather shoes. She stood in a patch of sunlight, the red blood under her shoes, the vivid carcasses stacked round her, a bullock bleeding its life away not six feet away from her, and the death-factory roaring all round her. She looked curiously, with hard, bold eyes, and was not afraid. (XXXV)

J. M. S. Tompkins comments on this passage that 'it is not often that we find sex and slaughter juxtaposed in Kipling's work, but when we do the effect is very violent and raw.'[17] But in stories like 'Beyond the Pale', 'On Greenhow Hill', and quite a number of others there is, if to a lesser degree, such a juxtaposition. The manner in which it is controlled can be related to the British experience of India both as a field of sexual promise and of violent action, just as the most remarkable and disturbing story that Kipling ever wrote in this vein, 'Mary Postgate' (1915) clearly gains its impetus from the bitter and devastating experience of the First World War. What is exceptional about the above passage is its sheer self-indulgence; the piling up of adjectives that suggests an undisciplined imitation of Wilde. In most of Kipling's fiction (*The Light That Failed*, his early novel, is an obvious exception the pace and brevity of the narrative imposes a valuable discipline.

That Kipling's attitude *is* a prurient one at times need not surprise us unduly, and we need to ask ourselves whether he is any more the 'knowing schoolboy' than, for example, Flaubert in his letters from Egypt. It is certainly true that he was rarely at ease with women. His warm recollection of the exceptional woman that he could talk to readily, like Mary Kingsley the explorer, tends to confirm this.[18] Certainly his handling of women characters in *The Light That Failed* is prurient and misogynistic by turns. The early 'smoking-room' label, however, was partly due to an uncertainty about quite where to place a writer as unusual as Kipling. With the publication of his *Barrack-Room Ballads* and some longer stories he became an important literary figure in his own right. It is in the longer stories of the early nineties rather than in the *Plain Tales* that his portrayal of sex and violence can be felt to be an integral part of his achievement. The sense of vulnerability in the young journalist foreshadows the capacity for pathos that emerges here. 'On Greenhow Hill' takes us some way beyond Kipling's career as an Anglo-Indian writer and into the period when he was becoming established in London, but this bleak tale of frustration and repression demonstrates quite strikingly how Kipling had learned to make use of India, and it shares with 'Beyond the Pale' the quality of masquerading as a romance rather than being one in any conventional sense.

The story in fact uses India solely as its framework, within which Private Learoyd tells the plaintive story of his home life in Yorkshire as a rough young miner, his wooing of a Methodist minister's daughter, her death of consumption, and his enlistment. At the heart of his tale however, the Yorkshire lead mines also represent the abyss that was central to the British experience of India. From the original Black Hole of Calcutta to the well-shafts into which the victims of the Mutiny were thrown to Amir Nath's gully, it is a recurring image, and it is repeated once again in the Marabar caves of *A Passage to India*. Yorkshire is explicitly aligned with India early on in the story: ' "It's along o' yon hill there", said Learoyd, watching the bare sub-Himalayan spur that reminded him of his Yorkshire moors.' But if the mine-working has implicit sexual overtones they are overwhelmed by violence here, as Learoyd plans the destruction of his rival for Liza's love: ' "I could take him a mile or two along th' drift, and leave him with his candle doused to cry hallelujah with none to hear him and say amen.... Niver a blasted leg to walk from Pateley. Niver an arm to put round Liza Roantree's waist. Niver no more – niver no more." ' The sense of overmastering desire that Learoyd's rhetoric generates is underscored by the narrator: 'The thick lips curled back over the yellow teeth, and that flushed face was not pretty to look upon', and it is echoed in the Indian frame, where 'the stillness of the wood and the desire of slaughter lay heavy on them.' But if the juxtaposition of sex and violence is still central to 'On Greenhow Hill' the world it describes is not over-simplified as a result. The brave little preacher who is Learoyd's rival is a fully drawn character, 'a little white-faced chap, wi a voice as 'ud wile a bird offan a bush', yet as deeply in love and determined in his suit as Learoyd, though able at the crisis to 'talk it all over quiet'. Compared with the rather insistent Kipling persona to whom we are accustomed, Learoyd's voice proves to be a remarkably sensitive instrument, and his own passion is skilfully modulated. When he is unable to kill the preacher and sets him down again, 'the' beck run stiller, an' there was no more buzzin' in my head like when th' bee come through th' window of Jesse's house.'

In a sense the world of the Yorkshire Methodists is the land of Learoyd's innocence, compared with the India in which he now finds himself, but it is also a land of more complex emotions than India seems able to allow. In India death becomes commonplace, and the story both opens and closes with the sound of a rifle-shot. The India of red, barren earth and kites is always in implicit contrast with the red cheeks and blue eyes, 'driven into pin-points by the wind', flagstone roofs and windhovers of Greenhow Hill. The scentless white violets that Learoyd roots up in his absorption symbolise an innocence that has become jaded rather than profitably replaced by experience. Ortheris's success in shooting the native deserter that rounds off the story is very clearly undercut by Learoyd's comment; 'Happen there was a lass tewed up wi' him, too.'

'On Greenhow Hill' goes well beyond specifically Anglo-Indian concerns and perspectives, but its poignancy is inseparable from the Indian frame. There is no indictment of Ortheris for looking on the deserter's death 'with the smile of the artist who looks on the completed work'. His is a job well done, but the long distance shot indirectly throws into relief the sense of distance and detachment that white men experience in India, and Learoyd's naive comment throws into further relief the contrast between the India on which the British are merely superimposed, and the richness of the home life. His story deals with feelings of loss and emotional exhaustion that India confirms. Compared with the attempt to use the native world as a romantic setting in 'Beyond the Pale' the indirect use of India here is a definite gain, for no considerations of race limit the depth of the Yorkshire setting. At the same time, however, the story withdraws from the tension between fear and desire that India could arouse. In fact the perspective of the barrack-room in all the soldier stories has the effect of distancing India to some extent, reducing it to a set of pressures that can be registered on their protagonists.

That Kipling should find ways of keeping India at some sort of distance is not really surprising. In fact it is more remarkable that its presence is actively felt in his work in ways other than the plain threat that had dominated British feelings since the Mutiny. There is an obvious parallel between upper-class Victorian Britain's growing concern about its industrial working class, and its fears of a recurrence of the Indian Mutiny. Distrust divided them from the new masses of population of the nineteenth century, whether industrial workers or the indigenous peoples of the Empire. In the case of Britain, the problem had been approached in the Industrial novels of Dickens, Mrs Gaskell, Disraeli, and George Eliot. Raymond Williams argues that

> These novels, when read together, seem to illustrate clearly enough not only the common criticism of industrialism, which the tradition was establishing, but also the general structure of feeling which was equally determining. Recognition of evil was balanced by fear of becoming involved. Sympathy was transformed, not into action, but into withdrawal.[19]

Kipling was writing both under the special conditions imposed by Anglo-India and at a later period when the withdrawal described by Raymond Williams was turning into reaction in Britain. His own approach to the British working classes will be the subject of later chapters. Fear of involvement is everywhere apparent in British writing on India, but the paradox in which it involves the ruling class is a good deal sharper; for in the Indian setting this fear is balanced not by recognition of industrial evils, but by thinly disguised desire for political and sexual possession. In this situation the latter cannot simply be dropped from the agenda when withdrawal turns into reaction. Thus, the reactionary voice is clear enough in 'The Head of the District', but it is also necessary that the Khursu Kheyl *enjoy* being dominated. It was possible, of course, to write of India without addressing the problem, and indeed it was the general practice. As Edward Said points out, every writer on the subject 'saw the Orient as a locale requiring Western attention, reconstruction, even redemption', and while this is an important element for Kipling too, it leaves ample scope for a merely homiletic fiction that does not attempt involvement at all.[20] By contrast Kipling's fiction frequently curtails, distances or moralises India, but it does not turn its back on it. Among the complex array of reasons for this, one of the most important is Kipling's particular vision of Empire. The British, he believed, must acquire a deeper and more intimate understanding of India. Part of the importance of his treatment of sex is that it acts as a metaphor for his social and political attitudes. In 'The Man Who Was' he remarks that 'Asia is not going to be civilised after the methods of the West. . . . You cannot reform a lady of many lovers, and Asia has been insatiable in her flirtations aforetime.' this is much in the manner of popular journalism in general, and Kipling's contributions are readily forgotten, as such generalisations rarely make for good fiction; but in some of his most powerful work the metaphor is a vehicle of real exploration.

For Kipling, there is obviously nothing evil about the system of Empire. Evil, where it exists, is squarely attributed to the Indians themselves. The idea of the dark abyss, of the malignant power, of chaotic lust and violence, are common to all colonial fiction. The white man is taken over by the 'horror' in Conrad's *Heart of Darkness*; the malignant devil of the South Seas is movable but indestructible in Robert Louis Stevenson's *The Bottle Imp*, and Flaubert uses an Oriental setting for the orgiastic violence of

Salammbo; but where these writers use the non-European setting to advantage, they also all universalise the 'evil force' with which they are dealing. In Kipling's work, by contrast, it has to be said that darkness and irrationality are confined to association with the native world. Jonah Raskin remarks that 'The things he admires and desires are repulsive and evil. Kipling accepted the values and judgements of the matron, his mother, but longed for a bohemian literature which would appeal to the prurient, and for romance with an Indian woman of passion'.[21] The element of truth in this needs considerable qualification, and it is the qualifications that are really important for an understanding of how Kipling's stories were produced. The attitude that is being castigated here is, in the first place, one that was shared by many other writers and artists at the time. Attitudes towards women were changing, under a host of influences that ranged from the invention of the safety bicycle to the plays of Ibsen, and 'bohemian' reactions to the old Victorian attitudes often descended into prurience. Such prurience is not, it should be said, always a feature of Kipling's work. 'On Greenhow Hill' is one example of his ability to handle strong desires with a maturity that accepts them as part of a broader pattern. Finally, it is impossible completely to disentangle Kipling's treatment of sex from his response to India and to the Empire. Like all Englishmen, he perceives a mystery in India which he desires to penetrate, but equally he believes, like all Englishmen, that to do so is to lose oneself. Another figure that fascinates him is the 'loafer' or white man 'gone native', like McIntosh Jellaludin in 'To be Filed for Reference', the last story in *Plain Tales*. McIntosh, it is hinted, has penetrated some of the mysteries of the East, but he pays the price in degradation and death. The brash young Kipling appears to promise us Jellaludin's 'manuscript' at a future date but, as with 'Mother Maturin', the promise was never fulfilled. Much as Kipling may have got to know India as a journalist, such a promise could never really be fulfilled, because India was understood to be necessarily alien and incomprehensible to Western minds; and as Kipling usually understood quite clearly, the Empire rested on a belief in that unbridgeable gulf. Yet it remains true that he, more than any other writer, explored the relationship between the British and India.

His early work reveals the element of a balancing act that he had to perform, as he makes an increasingly complex series of attempts to explore the effect of India as an active presence without losing the imperialist's sense of mission. India is an active presence in 'On Greenhow Hill', for the mine-working is an 'Indian' symbol of darkness and lust, but the displacement allows its emotional impact to be worked through. Here Learoyd accepts the darkness within himself and survives, where to imbibe the darkness of native India would be unthinkable. The value of this displacement becomes very evident when one looks at Kipling's early stories of 'native life', in the volume entitled *In Black and White* and elsewhere. Here the latent, unknowable quality of India that provides a tension is ignored in favour of the manifest intractability of Indians. Indian customs, Indian religions, Indian superstitions, throw up a bizarre problem which the white man proceeds to solve. The result may be quaint and exotic, and Kipling's contemporaries were duly impressed, but the *frisson* with which the Orient impinges on the white man's consciousness is gone. In the end Kipling was virtually to abolish evil in *Kim*, because his conception of evil remained too closely wedded to ideas about native 'ingratitude' that were a legacy of the Mutiny. To see India as a source of evil, however, implied that there was no prospect of the imperial harmony that he desired. The solution, in *Kim*, is to strike an optimistic note, but before he arrived at that, Kipling frequently expressed a despair that may be intensified by India, but which also reflects on the thinness of his own culture and civilisation. The case for his deeper vision, however, must follow on from a closer consideration of the ways in which Kipling used India throughout the eighteen-nineties.

3
Soldiers in India

> It's Oh to meet an Army man,
> Set up, and trimmed and taut,
> Who does not spout hashed libraries
> Or think the next man's thought,
> And walks as though he owned himself,
> And hogs his bristles short.

Soon after his return from India to London in 1889 Kipling wrote that 'The long-haired literati of the Savile Club are swearing that I 'invented' my soldier talk in *Soldiers Three*. Seeing that not one of these critters has been within earshot of a barrack, I am naturally wrath'.[1] He also wrote the set of verses bemoaning London to his friends in India, entitled 'In Partibus', of which the above is the final stanza. Kipling's affection for and devotion to the army in all its aspects was life-long. In his fiction the man who 'hogs his bristles short' is not always a paragon of virtue, but he can be forgiven almost anything but treachery, and this includes a certain amount of brutality, coldbloodedness, and even loss of nerve and running away. His irritation with the Savile Club literati is not directed so much at the assumption that his portraits of soldiers were not founded entirely on fact – they were not, as we shall see – as at the implication that he was exploiting a novelty rather than writing from personal sympathy. Kipling's very real interest in the army was certainly genuine, but his experience was limited to what he gathered from the officers and other ranks stationed at Fort Lahore. He possessed a ready ear and a devotion to the military virtues rather than much military knowledge. Certainly he had never seen the fighting in square in the Sudan, of which he wrote the remarkable description in *The Light That Failed* (1):

> The instinct of the desert, where there is always much war, told them that the right flank of the square was weakest, for they swung clear of the front. The camel-guns shelled them as they passed, and opened for an instant lanes through their midst, most

like those quick-closing vistas in a Kentish hop-garden seen when the train races by at full speed; and the infantry-fire, held till the opportune moment, dropped them in close-packed hundreds. No civilised troops in the world could have endured the hell through which they came, the living leaping high to avoid the dying who clutched at their heels, the wounded cursing and staggering forward, till they fell – a torrent black as the sliding water above a mill-dam – full on the right flank of the square. Then the line of the dusty troops and the faint blue desert sky overhead went out in rolling smoke, and the little stones on the heated ground and the tinder-dry clumps of scrub became matters of surpassing interest, for men measured their agonised retreat and recovery by these things, counting mechanically and hewing their way back to chosen pebble and branch.

His contemporaries, already astonished by what such a young man appeared to know, gaped again at this. It is a tour-de-force in which Kipling not only makes us believe that we are present, but in which he assembles many of his standard themes. There is the observation of the recklessness of the native warriors and their total disregard for life, which can serve both to legitimise the need for civilisation to be imposed, and to render a degree of 'uncivilised' behaviour on the part of British troops understandable. Sometimes fire has to be fought with fire, and a moment later one of Kipling's heroes removes the remains of an eyeball from his thumb. There is the nostalgia for England, the homesickness that occasionally descends on the warriors of the Empire – not expressed here, but embodied in the use of the hop-garden and the mill-dam as similes; and there is also the insistence, in the deliberately archaic 'most like', that soldiering in the Empire is always, even when the fragment before us is horrible, degrading, or even humorous, an epic business when properly understood. There is, finally, the climate and atmosphere of the lands 'East of Suez', whether India or the Egyptian desert. The whole Orient is a place where 'a man can raise a thirst', but also a place in which pressures unknown in England are brought to bear on the experienced and inexperienced alike, and where there is a constant struggle for the white man to keep his footing, a physical effort of 'counting mechanically and hewing their way back to chosen pebble and branch' which can have strange side-effects.[2] This is a strain imposed on all Kipling's white men, but on his soldiers par excellence.

For most readers of Kipling, to think of his soldiers will be to think of the common soldier in the barrack-room. Compared with the stories describing the escapades of Private Terence Mulvaney and his companions, those that deal with the officers tend to lack interest when they are not positively maudlin, and their heroes are ciphers. Young Bobby Wick's care of his men is rewarded with the epitaph 'bloomin' hangel' from one of them in 'Only A Subaltern'. Yet he is more memorable than most of Kipling's array of blue-eyed six-footers with names like 'Little Mildred', the 'Haileybury and Malborough chaps' who look forward to a proper 'row', and understate their blazing patriotism with a vocabulary full of ' 'Fraid' and 'Sha'n't '. His infatuation with phrases like 'sacrament of the mess' has become no easier to digest since they first appalled Lionel Johnson. With rather few exceptions, Kipling's obvious hero-worship lacks all control.

With the possible exception of Captain Gadsby, the most clearly individuated of this breed are two Georges – George Cottar in 'The Brushwood Boy' (1895), and the eponymous 'Georgie-Porgie'. The two appear to be linked together by the nursery rhymes used as story headings, both of which are apposite to their contrasting characters. If Kipling ever attempts seriously to examine the conflicting pulls on such men of the rural upper-class life of their parents and their experiences in India, it is in these two stories. Georgie Porgie is not a pleasant character, and his behaviour is completely condemned. He has married a Burmese girl and then coolly abandoned her, found himself a wife in England, and returned to India. The story ends as he and his new wife overhear the weeping of the Burmese girl Georgina, who has come to look for him, and suppose that 'some brute of a hillman has been beating his wife'. The irony is played out for all it is worth, with additional touches like the cheroots which Georgie Porgie used to share with Georgina, and are now banned from his new drawing-room. Although Kipling attacks one subaltern here, he does so with certain reservations, for Georgie Porgie is one of those indispensable men 'whose desire was to be ever a little in advance of the rush of Respectability'; a frontiersman who knows how to subdue a dacoit-infested jungle. There is a certain unfairness in expecting rigid moral standards of such a man. Where Georgie Porgie *is* attacked, for his cynicism, the attack is launched not solely on Georgina's behalf, but on behalf of his English wife. Georgie Porgie fails to 'rave, as do many bridegrooms, over the strangeness and delight of seeing his own true love sitting down to breakfast with him every morning. He had been there before, as the Americans say . . . '. It is this hypocrisy in respect of the much-idealised figure of the bride that may well have been most damning in the eyes of many of Kipling's readers. In the eyes of an observer Georgina is a 'poor little beast', in contrast with 'that angel', and Kipling has nothing further to say, other than to invite a little compunction on her behalf.

In 'The Brushwood Boy' the day is for duty, for George Cottar, the model professional soldier, and for his conventionally genteel beloved. The night is for their private, personal world; sentimentally in opposition to the day, but in reality complementing it. There is even an overlap, as this methodical Georgie makes a map of this dream-world, just as he would one of India's North-West Frontier. (Plate 6). Although some of his dreaming has the density and charm of childhood associations, at other times it functions as an allegory of Empire:

> Seeing the lily was labelled 'Hong Kong', Georgie said: 'Of course. This is precisely what I expected Hong Kong would be like. How magnificent!' Thousands of miles farther on it halted at yet another stone lily, labelled 'Java. . . . When his feet touched . . . that still water, it changed, with the rustle of unrolling maps, to nothing less than a sixth quarter of the globe, beyond the most remote imaginings of man – a place where islands were coloured yellow and blue, their lettering strung across their faces.

'Stone Lily' here is a rather splendid correlative for the 'collector's item' attitude of Imperialism towards its smaller possessions. After their dream has brought them together at last George's fiancée asks, 'but – what shall I do when I see you in the light?' It can only be inferred that she will submit to him lovingly, just as the Orient itself has done. In this story, however, both 'woman' and 'Orient' are lacunae defined by their opposites; by George himself, and by the loving description of his parents' home in England with its gamut of male preserves – trout streams, horses, dogs, and guns.

There is an obvious contrast between the fidelity of these two Georges, and it is no accident that George Cottar's more selfless passion coincides with a larger vision of Empire than Georgie Porgie achieves; but both stories portray the Orient as a field for energetic domination, sexual or political, and describe the restorative powers of leave in England when that energy is spent. If these stories about officers are written from an upper-class perspective, the same is, in the end, true of those concerned with the ordinary soldier. Accounts of Kipling's life and work have tended to assume the opposite by citing the popularity of these stories, and more particularly the *Barrack-Room Ballads*, with a mass audience. What is undoubtedly true is that these stories can still be enjoyed for the vigour with which the barrack-room is portrayed. In them Kipling accurately revealed for the first time the misery and boredom of the common soldier in India. Unlike his officers, his privates are enlivened by a fund of human frailty and error. They are disreputable, but more importantly they are vulnerable, and through the medium of their vulnerability some of the beauties and terrors of which India was composed for Kipling come to life.

He must certainly be given the credit for discovering the private soldier as a subject for fiction at an opportune moment. To the *Spectator*, Kipling's Tommy Atkins was 'a somewhat earthy personage on the whole, but with occasional gleams of chivalry and devotion lighting up his countenance.'[3] The review goes on to remark that Kipling avoids the tendency of 'realism' (as represented, presumably, by Zola) to portray the 'continuously animal', and it points out the wholesome balance struck by Kipling: 'The actualities of barrack-room life are not extenuated, but the tone of the whole is sound and manly.' The actuality was that the Tommy of Kipling's day was recruited from the very lowest classes of society, the unskilled and the destitute. Being in the army did not raise him above his origins in the eyes of his compatriots, and the Cockney soldier of Kipling's stories and ballads complains more than once of being ejected from public houses that considered themselves respectable. In caste-ridden India these other ranks were catered for, but even more socially isolated. The rising tide of the 'New Imperialism' did, however, furnish an opportunity for the soldier to rival the sailor as a popular favourite. It was the army that was producing the heroes of the day in Gordon, Wolseley, and Lord Roberts: Martyr, Strategist, and Man of the People respectively. Charles Carrington remarks that there is 'no adequate account of the British soldier, what he thought of his officers, and what he talked about the night before the battle, between Shakespeare's *Henry V* and Kipling's *Barrack-Room Ballads*'.[4] It is indeed true that there was a similar chasm between the social positions of nobility and peasants, officers and other ranks, in Kipling's time as in

Shakespeare's. His trio of soldiers do frequently remind one of Shakespearian 'mechanicals', and this is helpful as a means of establishing them in the reader's affections. The authorial perspective that it implies, however, is one to be borne in mind when considering the kind of 'journalistic' realism that Kipling also appears to be claiming. The most obvious device in *Soldiers Three* does indeed take us back to *Henry V*. It is the employment of three 'regional' characters speaking in dialect, and engaging in exchanges in which their regional traits are in themselves the basis for humorous contrast and conflict. Instead of Fluellen and company, Kipling offers Learoyd, the slow-moving, forceful Yorkshireman; Mulvaney, the silver-tongued, roguish, sentimental Irishman; and Ortheris, the sharp-witted, pert, cynical Cockney.

Of the three it is Mulvaney who bulks the largest and who has commanded almost all the critical attention. The stories he tells, often about himself, depend heavily for their effect on the interpolations of Ortheris, and it is in two stories in which Ortheris is the central figure that we can observe most clearly both the relationship of narrator and characters and the careful construction by Kipling of his picture of army life. It is through Ortheris rather than the more complex and 'dispershed' figure of Mulvaney that Kipling offers the public the 'typical' private of the line.

A striking feature of all the stories about the 'Soldiers Three' is their relationship with the 'I' who tells the tale. Some care is taken to make the acquaintance credible. It is mentioned that the three are initially suspicious of a 'bloomin' civilian',[5] and it is made clear that their meetings with him depend on the chance crossings of paths in the course of work. It is a happy encounter across social barriers which work can sometimes help to relax. As it is not sustained it does not challenge overmuch the conventional distance between classes, though we may wonder whether Kipling raised one or two contemporary eyebrows with the statement that it was 'better to sit out with Mulvaney than to dance many dances'.[6] Crucial to the relationship is the mutual respect of each for the other's station in life. 'I' is always addresssed by Mulvaney as 'Sorr', but in military matters he is the respectful novice –

'Begin at the beginning and go on to the end', I said royally. 'But rake up the fire a bit first.'
I passed Ortheris's bayonet for a poker.
'That shows how little we know what we do', said Mulvaney,

putting it aside. 'Fire takes all the heart out av the steel, an' the next time, may be, that our little man is fighting for his life his bradawl'll break, an' so you'll ha' killed him, manin' no more than to kape yourself warm. 'Tis a recruity's thrick that. Pass the clanin' rod, sorr.'

I snuggled down abashed; and after an interval the voice of Mulvaney began . . .[7]

An early satire of Kipling in *Punch* ignores this mutual respect. To see the delicate balance trampled on makes one realise how carefully Kipling sustains it:

'Really, O'Rammis,' I ventured to observe, for I noticed that he and his two friends had pulled all the other five bottles out of my pocket, and had finished them. 'I'm a little disappointed with you today. I came out here for a little quiet blood-and-thunder before going to bed, and you are mixing up your stories like the regimental laundress's soapsuds.'[8]

But in the passage about the bayonet above, the use of the narrator is most effective. Social status is at its least important in the darkness around the camp-fire, and the little aside becomes emblematic of the glories and dangers of soldiering: literally, of fire and sword. Kipling manages to convey this with the antithesis of a 'blood-and-thunder' style. In the two stories concerning Ortheris the subject is not the soldier's hardships so much as necessary discipline, and Kipling finds himself in need of a rather more strenuous narrative technique.

'The Madness of Private Ortheris' is one of the earliest of the stories about the trio. It is also one of the most frequently referred to by critics and reviewers of the nineties, and one can sense in their reaction a feeling that Kipling has convincingly 'hit off' an aspect of the Tommy's life. The opening lines establish very clearly the relationship of 'I' and the soldiers, as well as swiftly differentiating the characters of Mulvaney and Ortheris.

They sent me an invitation to join them, and were genuinely pained when I brought beer – almost enough beer to satisfy two Privates of the Line . . . and Me.

' 'Twasn't for that we bid you welkim, Sorr,' said Mulvaney sulkily. ' 'Twas for the pleasure av your comp'ny.'

Ortheris came to the rescue with – 'Well, 'e won't be none the worse for bringing liquor with 'im. We ain't a file of Dooks.'

A familiar note throughout Kipling's early work is his ironic indication of the privations of India: 'We shot all the forenoon, and killed two pariah-dogs, four green parrots, sitting, one kite by the burning-ghaut, one snake flying, one mud-turtle, and eight crows. Game was plentiful.' Ortheris's 'madness' arises from the aimless and tawdry existence implied here. It consists in an overwhelming homesickness and self-reproach for being a mere soldier, and it crescendoes into a magnificent soliloquy which is the more striking for being placed at the centre of a very short story:

'Now I'm sick to go 'Ome – go 'Ome! No, I ain't mammysick, because my uncle brung me up, but I'm sick for London again; sick for the sounds of 'er, an' the sights of 'er, and the stinks of 'er; orange peel and hasphalte an' gas comin' in over Vaux'all Bridge. Sick for the rail goin' down to Box 'Ill, with your gal on your knee an' a new clay pipe in your face. That, an' the Stran' lights where you knows ev'ry one, an' the Copper that takes you up is a old friend that tuk you up before, when you was a little, smitchy boy lyin' loose 'tween the Temple an' the Dark Harches. No bloomin' guard-mountin', no bloomin' rotten-stone, nor khaki, an' yourself your own master with a gal to take an' see the Humaners practisin' a-hookin' dead corpses out of the Serpentine o' Sundays. An' I lef' all that for to serve the Widder beyond the seas, where there ain't no women and there ain't no liquor worth 'avin', and there ain't nothin' to see, nor do, nor say, nor feel, nor think. Lord love you Stanley Orth'ris, but you're a bigger bloomin' fool than the rest of the reg'ment and Mulvaney wired together! There's the Widder sittin' at 'Ome with a gold crownd on 'er 'ead; and 'ere am Hi, Stanley Orth'ris, the Widder's property, a rottin' FOOL!'

Discontent with Victoria R. I., Queen of England and Empress of India, 'the Widder', is rare among Kipling's soldiers. The only parallel to Ortheris's sentiments comes from the speaker of 'The Widow at Windsor', who has had enough for the time being of sentry-go across the world. His inability to escape the bugles' call is robustly put in these lines:

> Take 'old o' the Wings o' the Mornin',
>   An' flop round the earth till you're dead;
> But you won't get away from the tune that they play
>   To the bloomin' old rag over'ead.

The effect in both cases, however, is to make us feel that the soldier who speaks with the unconscious vigour of the latter or the sensuous rhythms of the former is not likely to brood upon injustices. Indeed, Ortheris's eloquent nostalgia literally thrusts to the margins his real insight that he is the 'Widder's property'. His speech bestows on him a qualified, 'working-man's' dignity, based on his ability to value the simple pleasures of life. That those simple pleasures are *not* likely to be those of Kipling and his readers is underscored by the pastimes selected. One genuinely false note is surely the statement that 'the Copper that takes you up is a old friend'. This is surely true of the Copper who takes 'I' up, as in 'Brugglesmith', rather than of Ortheris, who rarely sentimentalises authority in this fashion. He has no need to, for below his surface discontent there is a doglike devotion. After being allowed to don civilian clothes and being left in isolation he is relieved to feel the rasp of his army shirt again, and 'The devils had departed from Private Stanley Ortheris, No. 22639, B company.' For as Kipling rather baldly explains, 'God in His wisdom has made the heart of the British Soldier, who is very often an unlicked ruffian, as soft as the heart of a little child.' The story is exceptionally revealing of the underlying class relationship because, uniquely, 'I' is an active participant. Elsewhere Kipling made his narrator a mere recorder of events, possibly lest he himself should do to his 'Soldiers Three' what the satire in *Punch* had done to them.

From the point of view of Kipling's 'realistic' contrivances, 'His Private Honour' is, in essence, 'The Madness of Private Ortheris' turned inside out. In the latter Ortheris's long speech in the middle of the tale gives him a dignity which turns out to be conditional on his remaining exactly where he is. In 'His Private Honour' it is the final page which allows Ortheris to assert his dignity, while the tale's central set-piece sets out the conditions in which he possesses it. The narrator dreams of a much enlarged army in India which will settle there permanently and breed more Indian-born white soldiers, 'and perhaps a second fighting-line of Eurasians'. This dream has been considered artistically objectionable, but its function is to lend a necessary grandeur to the army which will justify the harsh business of breaking-in the new recruits.[9] At the end of the story when Ortheris asserts himself in these terms – 'My Right! I ain't a recruity to go whinin' about my rights to this an' my rights to that, just as if I couldn't look after myself. My rights! 'Strewth A'mighty! I'm a man.' – we are apt to forget the rather chilling fact that it is the unfortunate recruit Anderson, the uncomprehending outlet for Ortheris's rage at being struck by his officer, who stands as a negative example here. Ortheris nicknames him 'Samuelson', after which it is noticeable that the narrator also refers to him as Samuelson but without, as it were, the inverted commas. Ortheris's sense of dignity here actually depends on an acceptance of illegal violence; bullying, in fact. The point, for Kipling, is that everyone in the story, from officers down to new recruits are serving the larger purposes of the Empire. Nor is the vision the narrator has altogether a dream. Kipling is certainly original and even provocative in proposing an Indian-based army with a Eurasian component, but the idea of an empire guarding its own outposts and directing its mixed population at will is part and parcel of the 'New Imperialism' propounded by Seeley, Rhodes, and Chamberlain; and their ideas appeared at the time to be almost accomplished fact.[10] It was to be several years before Max Beerbohm depicted Kipling having 'A day out with Britannia'.[11] Here Kipling seems to offer us almost his caricature self in the figure warming himself on the cannon overlooking the parade-ground, and making his imaginary map of the Empire.

The stories that feature Ortheris are revealing of the upper-class standpoint from which Kipling is really writing, and which is in fact one of the literary conventions that the reader accepts. The whole point about Mulvaney in particular is that he is a private of the line, and very precisely that. We are often reminded that he has been reduced from the rank of a corporal. His wisdom and virtue operate within strict limits, and the world as seen by Mulvaney is a view of whose distortions we are conscious. His is a submerged angle of vision, not the 'true' horizontal of reader and narrator. Mulvaney is such a large and influential figure that it is important to realise that he is nevertheless as much a 'mechanical' as Bottom or Dogberry. In a lower key he shares their absurd naivety; his horrified innocence, for example, when confronted with erotic Indian sculpture, or his ignorance of the significance of locomotor attacks. Henry James recognised this true status when he described him as having 'the tongue of a hoarse syren and . . . mysteries and infinitudes almost Carlylese.' Such mysteries and infinitudes are not to be taken too seriously. In practice the serious side of Mulvaney can be summarised by the narrator in a single sentence from 'The Courting of Dinah Shadd': 'I knew that he was a man of inextinguishable sorrow.'

Life within an Indian barracks is pictured in one of its most complete forms in this story, and the pathos of Mulvaney's tale is powerfully enhanced by the muddy and angular cantonment setting. There is a degree of pathos inherent in the way in which the world of the Irish soldiers looks inwards on itself without being able to escape the influence of the oriental world surrounding it. Mulvaney's courtship might, in one sense, take place in an Irish village, for all the principal characters are Irish 'types'. In the framework of the story's present, the euphoric atmosphere of the camp-fires contrasts with Mulvaney's troubled history to make a bittersweet whole. The depths of India that the story makes no attempt to explore still encircle it with their influence like the stars above the camp: 'Over our heads burned the wonderful Indian stars, which are not all pricked in on one plane, but, preserving an orderly perspective, draw the eye through the velvet darkness of the void up to the barred door of heaven itself.' The perspective of the barracks puts the Indian world at a distance, but the pressures of life in India do not fall away; and the lives of Kipling's soldiers are tailored to bring them into play. In this case it is the fatal cholera that stalks the tranquil scene.

The absence of a more concretely 'Indian' setting might suggest that the Mulvaney stories are written from a specifically 'Anglo-Indian' viewpoint rather than to present the vicarious 'picture-book' Orient that might appeal to the English reader; but the perspective is one that transfers the outlook of the upper strata of Anglo-India onto the world of the private soldier in order to dramatise and romanticise India in a new way. The lower ranks of the army were actually in much closer contact with the 'natives' than Kipling leads us to suppose. In 1893, for example

> The main military brothel at Lucknow cantonment was a substantial building. In Indian style there were two courtyards, with fifty-five rooms opening onto them. Mrs Andrews described the matron of the Lancers' brothel as a very prosperous person wearing 'a great deal of solid gold jewellery.' She was also 'a fine-looking woman, that is', added Mrs Andrews grudgingly, 'judging by the native type.'

The Lancers' matron was on intimate terms with a British NCO, Orderly Sgt Edward Theobald. She referred to him as her husband, and he signed his letters 'Your loving husband'.[12]

While Kipling deals, in a handful of stories, with love affairs between white civilians and native women, he keeps his soldiers free of any such taint, and never refers to the kind of daily contact that a regimental brothel would imply. Mulvaney seeks sexual gratification in the married quarters, and not only Mulvaney; in two other stories such philandering leads to murder and punishment. This is not to say that Kipling could or should have written about the lal bazaars. Andrew Lang, one of his earliest supporters, evidently found 'Love-o'-Women' repellent because it touched upon this subject.[13] Whether conscious or unconscious, the 'censorship' is part of the pattern to which Kipling shapes India for his readers. His 'realism' involves selecting from the reality so as to present life in India as one of extremes, extreme beauty and extreme harshness; while the native world, and in particular native women, are to be explored at one's peril. We hear scarcely anything, either, of the native servants that even private soldiers employed to look after their uniforms and run errands. In the one story in which Mulvaney does encounter Indian women, 'The Incarnation of Krishna Mulvaney', the meeting is subject to stringent controls.

The story is one of Kipling's farces, but at its core is Mulvaney's experience in the temple of Prithi-Devi:

> Thin a man began to sing an' play on somethin' back in the dhark, an' twas a queer song. Ut made my hair lift on the back av my neck. Thin the doors av all the palanquins slid back, an' the women bundled out. I saw what I'll niver see again. 'Twas more glorious than thransformations at a pantomime, for they was in pink an' blue an' silver an' red an' grass-green, wid diamonds an' imralds an' great red rubies all over thim. But that was the least part av the glory. O bhoys, they were more lovely than the like of any loveliness in hiven; ay, their little bare feet were better than the white hands of a lord's lady, an' their mouths were like puckered roses, an' their eyes were bigger an' dharker than the eyes av any livin' women I've seen. Ye may laugh, but I'm speakin' truth. I niver saw the like, an' niver will again.

What follows, dealing with Mulvaney's extrication of himself by impersonating Krishna and his return to camp serves, like the nonsensical plot that precedes it, to qualify, and almost to deny the experience. Mulvaney's voice is used to masterly effect to lend an air of awestruck innocence to the highly-wrought, sensuous description of the women. At the same time all this loveliness is conveyed with a muffled intensity which reminds us that behind it lies the gross erotic sculpture of the archway to the temple. Mulvaney becomes Krishna for a moment, or rather Krishna becomes Mulvaney, but he is also a common soldier, and a drunken one at that. To have him stumble in this condition upon a Queen's praying at Benares heightens the deeply attractive scene, but then isolates it from normal life. Mulvaney is very firmly guided back to regimental reality and to his proper role in life which is to 'teach the new recruits how to "Fear God, Honour the Queen, Shoot Straight, and Keep Clean." ' This emphatic control only reinforces our sense that Oriental beauty always has, for Kipling, an implicit power to disturb.

This power is everywhere apparent in 'Love-o'-Women', whose dazzling opening paragraph creates a 'realistic' Indian setting par excellence – hot, dusty, and strange; made for violence and hysteria. We scarcely notice, as the focus narrows onto the courtroom through the physical details of tikka-gharri (a small cart) and flapping punkah, the absence of any Indians. Descriptions are starkly vivid at every turn; the language of both the narrator and Mulvaney is rhetorically heightened throughout; and yet its subject is the decay of a man dying of syphilis, framed by the ostensibly dreary and commonplace incident of a shooting in barracks. J. F. Fenwick has argued that the 'frame' is too heavy, drawing attention away from the main story,[14] but 'Love-o'-Women' relies on a brilliant impressionistic tableau of 'India' to which both story and frame contribute. Among the whole series of tableaux through which the story moves it is the opening of the 'frame' and the central moment in the 'story' that most complement each other. Mulvaney, in the latter, returns us to the same emotional pitch with which the narrator opens:

> The horror, the confusion, and the separation of the murderer from his comrades were all over before I came. There remained only on the barrack-square the blood of man calling from the ground. The hot sun had dried it to a dusky goldbeater's skin film, cracked lozenge-wise by the heat; and as the wind rose, each lozenge, rising a little, curled up at the edges as if it were a dumb

tongue. Then a heavier gust blew all away down wind in grains of dark-coloured dust. It was too hot to stand in the sunshine before breakfast. The men were in barracks talking the matter over. A knot of soldiers' wives stood by one of the entrances to the married quarters, while inside a woman shrieked and raved with wicked filthy words.

I cud see that the two was in the verandah where I'd left them, an' I knew by the hang av her head an' the noise av the crows fwhat had happened. 'Twas the first and the last time that I'd iver known woman to use the pistol. They fear the shot as a rule, but Di'monds-an'-Pearls she did not – she did not.

The parallel between the gentleman-ranker and his mistress and Antony and Cleopatra is indeed appropriate, for like *Antony and Cleopatra*, 'Love-o'-Women' relies on a language that can hold the tragic and the farcical in suspense. The 'dumb tongues' weave themselves in and out of Mulvaney's tenacious eloquence.

Mulvaney himself is set here on a wider stage than usual. He commands easily among his fellow-privates, his audience, but we are strongly aware of his limited angle of vision and his lack of education. Not only the narrator, but Dr Lowndes and 'Love-o'-Women' himself are gentlemen, and their presence exposes Mulvaney as slightly naive. He sems not quite to grasp the full significance of everything he reports, and the reader makes some connections, as it were, for him. On the other hand the asides about the dead man being in Hell, and Mulvaney's role as a kind of father-confessor, do more than reveal him as Irish and working-class. That Hell in this story is real is a point on which the narrator and Mulvaney undoubtedly concur, and the tale that each tells points the same grim moral. The thought that India itself is a kind of hell: hot, dusty, and full of torments, is never far away, and neither is the thought that it is also a female entity which taxes and lays waste the strength of men.

Both the lucid journalist-narrator and Mulvaney are portrayed as 'insiders', describing things with which they are familiar, and both use similes which flash an alien, exotic India at us:

The judge put his hand to his brow before giving sentence, and the Adam's apple in the prisoner's throat went up and down like mercury pumping before a cyclone.

Thin he fired again, an' that dhrew a fresh volley, and the long
slugs that they chew in their teeth came floppin' among the rocks
like tree toads av a hot night.

This turning to the Orient itself for similes, when, as in the
comparison of the regiment in square to a Kentish hop-garden in
The Light That Failed, Kipling often does the opposite, indicates a
strategy. The whole story seeks to create an India that is both
extraordinary and that provides an enclosed space conducive to
tragic intensity: a setting in which it is possible for the diseased
soldier to exclaim to his 'Di'monds an' Pearls', 'I'm dyin', Aigypt,
dyin' '. Essential to the atmosphere is the focus on woman as the
'poisoned cup', which is constantly intensified. All the figures in
the story are philanderers. Mulvaney himself has been one, the
doctor who attends Love-'o-Women is about to run off with another
man's wife, and one of the soldiers in Mulvaney's guard tries to
sneak off to the bazaar even as the story is being told. The murderer
in the 'frame' is an outraged husband whose wife we hear
'shrieking and raving with wicked filthy words'. The faithful Dinah
is no more than a skilful piece of counterpoint as the tale builds
towards its climax. When Di'monds an' Pearls appears, Mulvaney's
description embodies an attitude that the entire story serves: 'The
red paint stud lone on the white av her face like a Bull's eye on a
target.' Sex and violence are fused again here, but in this setting the
fusion seems natural enough. Love-o'-Women is not, like Learoyd
in 'On Greenhow Hill', a fully realised character; he is, like
Mephistopheles, in hell already. He is held up as a warning, but the
dazzling and sinister India through which he moves seems to
threaten us all.

In this respect it is important that he is dying from syphilis, for
the story's infernal and romantic aspects are ballasted by Kipling's
polemic against public attitudes towards the disease. He was
'outraged that it was considered impious that the disease-riddled
prostitutes of the bazaar should be medically inspected.'[15] His
anger, in fact, was caused by the suspension of the Indian
Contagious Diseases Act of 1868 and its replacement with a new,
vaguely worded Cantonments Act in 1889. The pressure that
brought about this change was the knock-on effect on the Raj of
Josephine Butler's famous and successful campaign for the repeal of
the English Contagious Diseases Act, which did away with the
forcible medical inspections of the innumerable working-class

women whom the authorities considered to be prostitutes. It is not hard to imagine Kipling's contempt for the Indian administrators who bowed to such pressure. He certainly had strong feelings derived from his first-hand observation of the misery caused: new measures were in fact to be introduced to combat the situation in 1896, when it became known that over half the British Army in India were suffering from venereal disease.

To critics who found his tale simply too lurid, Kipling could thus reply that he had a practical aim in view. But from the distance of a hundred years we can surely see something contradictory in a story which addresses itself to a social problem and yet romanticises its subject to such an intense degree. Love-o'-Women is dying not only from syphilis but from heart-broken remorse; indeed the former – such is the effect of Mulvaney's picturesque language and double-edged naiveté – seems almost to be a symptom of the latter. There is a contradiction between the stern warning against deviation from acceptable sexual norms and the element of voyeurism with which the tragedy is witnessed.

It is important to be aware that the voyeuristic element had its advantages in the market-place. Fictional interest in 'unconvention' women was blossoming in the early nineties. On the highest plane Ibsen's work was becoming known, and Hardy's *Tess of the D'Urbervilles* and Pinero's *The Second Mrs Tanqueray* were seriously challenging the presuppositions of their audiences. Not all work that exploited a similar 'interest' did anything of the kind. More relevant here is a play like Charles Haddon Chambers's *The Idler* (1891). Here the innocent female victim Helen Harding is surrounded by a trio of men who have 'sown their wild oats' to the extent that her husband Sir John Harding MP is, under the name of 'Gentleman Jack', still wanted for murder in the American West. In fact Helen only risks compromising herself for the sake of her husband, and her honour is saved when at the last moment the three gentlemen resolve their differences like gentlemen. The 'Idler' of the title also chooses an honourable remedy for his disappointed love – he undertakes an expedition to the North Pole. It is a play that sets out to titillate his audience, not to shock or challenge it. While various forms of misalliance become a favoured topic, the proposed solution was less often that women deserved to be treated differently, and more that men must not be tempted to behave like 'cads'. Within that framework a degree of risky courage and independent action, *pace* Helen Harding, could be applauded. No doubt some men were growing a little tired of the totally subservient 'Angel in the House'.

Meanwhile the 'New Woman' who sought to challenge existing mores could be tolerated, patronised, and even valued for the voyeuristic excitement that her flouting of convention could provide. That least lovable of critics and reviewers, Robert Buchanan, who was to attack Kipling's 'hooliganism' as he had Rossetti's 'degeneracy', with impartial vindictiveness, probably voices in the blatantly hypocritical journalese of his contribution to *The New Fiction* (1895) an attitude unconsciously adopted by many.[16]

> The New Woman, eager to prove her capacity for independence, for a life parallel with and equal to the life of man, seizes the subject which lies nearest to her knowledge, that of sex, and reveals, even in her moments of utter impropriety, something that is individual. . . . When Ophelia recovers her reason, which she will most certainly do, she may be a little shocked. . . . Let us be content to lose our superstitions concerning her, to accept her as she is, in all her honest and thoroughgoing nudity; and in the meantime let us welcome her pretty improprieties as a valuable revelation.

It is evidently possible both to speak of women in the most patronising way and yet to welcome the disappearance of the Victorian code which insisted that women were to be protected as repositories of society's values. The portrayal in some novels of the nineties of women flouting convention, refusing to submit to marriage, and actually exercising their sexual preferences, is only welcomed as increasing the field of male opportunity. The shift in attitude from a Patmore to a Buchanan might even be seen as belonging to the same 'structure of feeling' that was also eroding the sense of paternal obligation that the British felt towards other races. If women and 'natives' could both be regarded as types of property, might it not be natural enough for the individual whose sense of 'ownership' was not very secure to reinforce it by using his strength to abuse or degrade them? It is worth making, at least, the general point that this was a period in which a social system geared to the protection of property was becoming an encumbrance and a strain on the young man of the middle class who was supposed to benefit from it, but found himself without sufficient means to make good; and unable, in particular, to enter into marriage. Absurdly long engagements were not uncommon. We know that gentlemen's clubs and prostitution both flourished as a result, but we can hardly suppose that they overcame the basic sense of frustration. To take this view, however, is to point out that responses to it could vary considerably. Not every reaction was of Buchanan's type, and Lionel Trilling's famous remark that Kipling's work reverberates with a 'lower-middle-class snarl of defeated gentility' has the unfairness of any gross oversimplification.[17] There is an element of sexual fantasy in 'Love-o'-Women' as in some of Kipling's other stories, and the soldier is in many ways a convenient alter ego for Kipling's readership, but the despair and the compassion that are aroused are not completely invalidated by this. Although India seems to be not merely the setting but the catalyst for the disaster, there is no simple allocation of blame. The association between the 'unfairness' of India and the 'unfairness' confronting the young gentleman of the period is used with varying degrees of success. The latter can never be very openly expressed, and indeed breaches of the social code have to be condemned. 'Georgie Porgie' shows Kipling's wavering between sympathy for red blood and concern for moral rectitude at its crudest. In 'Love-o'-Women' a similar ambivalence is expressed with imagination of a different quality. He explores the dilemmas as well as the fantasies of his male readership, and if the character he creates is outlandish and melodramatic, the dangers of contracting syphilis could be feared by everyone.

Neither the fact that Kipling was an Anglo-Indian, nor his personal interest in the private soldier, prevent him from sharing and reflecting the attitudes and concerns of his period, his sex, or his social class. It is such a common conception of Kipling that his Indian background made him a unique figure in the nineties that it is important to stress how relevant his work was to contemporary issues and moods. At the same time as he plays up the 'mechanical' side of Mulvaney he invests him with the perspectives of the ruling class. It is interesting to note how fragments of the underworld really inhabited by soldiers in India float through the stories occasionally like harmless microbes, without disturbing their intended current. In 'Love-o'-Women' a soldier does attempt to sneak off to the bazaar, but the story ignores such mundane sexual activity in favour of the explosive passion of the white man and his white woman. In 'The Big Drunk Draf'' the British soldier's propensity for looting and rape is casually mentioned. These are aspects of the behaviour of the British soldier in India on which Kipling not only prefers not to dwell, but for which he has no literary use. The occasional outbursts of violence that afflicted the soldier in barracks are another matter. A remarkable feature of the soldier stories as a group is the frequency with which the incident of a shooting in barracks is used. It is the subject of 'In the Matter of a Private' and 'Black Jack' as well as providing the frame for 'Love-o'-Women'. A scene in 'In the Matter of a Private' almost re-enacts one of the most famous incidents of the Mutiny, the shooting of General Hearsey who, like Kipling's Major Oldyne, refused to take cover; but less than this is sufficient to bring memories of the Mutiny into play. In Kipling's stories, of course, it is white soldiers who are running amok under the intolerable strain of their lives; but we are conscious, as always, that irrational violence is to be expected in the Orient. Even white soldiers may be a threat, and the affection in which Kipling's 'three musketeers' are held does not disguise a continual insistence on the need for instilling the right spirit into the ranks, backed by strong discipline. As if to reassure himself on this score Kipling also wrote the absurd, if grim, account of how a loyal regiment deals with a Fenian agent-provocateur in 'The Mutiny of the Mavericks'. Ortheris and Mulvaney themselves behave in ways that could be a threat to discipline if taken to extremes. Mulvaney is frequently locked up for drunken disorderliness, but more importantly he functions as a 'safe' version of Love-o'-Women, just as Ortheris's madness is a 'safe' version of that of Simmons in 'In the Matter of a Private'. Kiplings real affection for the common soldier is affection for the man who, by and large, submits cheerfully to rigorous discipline. Precisely because private soldiers are such an isolated and strictly regulated group they have a good deal of freedom to speak and think as they please.

Such freedom is appropriate to the clown, and it is because of his comic potential as well as his ability to moralise that Mulvaney tends to dominate in the soldier stories. Part schemer, part buffoon, and often the victim of improbable circumstances, he is first and foremost a loveable rogue, though like all good clowns he has his sorrowful side. The originality of Kipling's Indian settings led many to think in terms of a deeper kind of comedy; for Kipling had not only created a larger-than-life character, but appeared to have a new social world to explore. His early reviewers often found themselves reminded of Dickens, and Henry James was even moved to think of Balzac.[18] To his reading public generally Kipling was undoubtedly a 'realist', in that he was more than willing to concede that his soldiers stole dogs and drank too heavily, and that the work they were employed to do was 'butcher's work'. 'Butcher and bolt' was a common nickname for the punitive expeditions of the British Army in India. To be a realist was also to write 'strong stuff', and Kipling's taut, elliptical manner of portraying violence, as in a much-quoted sentence from 'With the Main Guard' – ' "Tim Coulan'll slape easy tonight", ses he wid a grin; an' the next minut his head was in two halves and he wint down grinnin' by sections.' – made a powerfull impression. Wide though the differences are, it is hardly surprising that Kipling's combinations of the grim and the whimsically grotesque should have brought Dickens to mind. We have, however, to accept that Mulvaney's performances do not challenge any presuppositions or imply any serious criticism of a world in which everyone's place is known and numbered. As Adrian Poole has put it, Kipling's work lacks the educative process at work in a Dickens novel,[19] and this is readily to be seen in the homogeneous group of stories concerning the 'Soldiers Three', whose overall project is to celebrate the strength in vicissitude of the army that guards the Empire, and which ultimately acknowledges no higher virtue than to 'shoot straight and honour the Queen'.

Mulvaney and his companions do, however, represent an important development in Kipling's literary use of India. They are, of course, mythological creatures, but it is precisely those characteristics which make them appear refreshingly 'realistic' – their familiarity with violence and bloodshed, the presentation of their surroundings as hostile and enervating, and their sexual latitude – through which Kipling can channel an image of 'India' that will appeal above all to a male, middle-class English readership. If he can be seen on the one hand to be shrewdly tailoring his fiction for such an audience, the barrack-room is fully enough realised to encourage reflection on the kind of life it permits. Like the drawing-room the barrack-room has both its decorum and its routines. The freedom from its restraints that is enjoyed in Mulvaney's comic escapades obviously does no harm, but we are frequently aware of the potential dangers that accompany such freedom. Like the drawing-room of social drama the barrack-room is also an institution isolated from the outside world, but subject to powerful pressures from it, although Kipling is concerned to defend rather than to attack the institution. As Mulvaney keeps a fatherly eye on his younger comrades, it is his earthy wisdom and good sense, and his acceptance of authority, which prevail. But if the pressures and temptations that India creates are treated with hostility they are still keenly felt, and the soldier's dull round is capable of exploding into tragedy too. If the individuals who are destroyed are portrayed as weak or wanton, there is pity for their inability to cope with that pressure. The potential violence and the sexual promise inherent in the 'India' of these stories is always felt to be active. Even in the more idyllic moments there is a sense of India constantly stirring: 'The earth was a grey shadow more unreal than the sky. We could hear her breathing lightly in the pauses between the howling of the jackals, the movement of the wind in the tamarisks, and the fitful mutter of musketry-fire leagues away to the left.'[20] For Kipling, as I have already argued, British rule over India necessitated a fulness of possession that required full-blooded involvement. The soldier stories keep India out of the foreground, but its constant presence means that the constraints of the barrack-room also reflect the irksome nature of a Raj isolated from its subjects. In the end Mulvaney's geniality is in striking contrast with the dark and troubled world he often inhabits.

Two of the largest projects within Kipling's fiction about India, the soldier stories and *Kim*, also present a striking contrast. In the former Indian beauty, savagery, despair, secrete themselves in the tales; the latter seeks to embrace and explore India in its entirety. A concretely sensuous India emerges from both, but in very different lights. In attempting to construct the vision of Empire which always informs his work, and which finds its final expression in *Kim*, Kipling occasionally presented India through the medium of a story which is overtly presented as a significant legend or myth. This is the approach most successfully adopted in 'The Man Who Would Be King'; a story which takes the adventurous spirit of Mulvaney one stage further.

The story's protagonists, Dravot and Carnehan, are not regular soldiers but 'loafers'; that is, white men without regular employment or official positions. Such men were an anomaly and sometimes an embarrassment in India's tightly organised white enclaves, and were regarded as vagabonds probably given over to alcoholism and liaisons with native women. Kipling had described one loafer in 'To be Filed for Reference', but had not told the story of his life. As he makes Jellaludin remark of his putative autobiography, 'Some of it must go; the public are fools, and prudish fools'. Now, in the last story he wrote in India, he found another way of using this character. The absurd but compelling logic behind 'The Man Who Would Be King' is that Dravot and Carnehan, being white men without occupation, will occupy themselves by adding an entire new country to the Empire. Kipling situates this country in the almost uncharted region between the northern borders of Afghanistan and Tibet, which was the scene of some legendary exploits by scouts from the Indian Army's intelligence section, and a place that held almost the same kind of fascination for Victorians as the Upper Nile. If its name, 'Kafiristan', has any significance, it is to suggest that this is entirely virgin territory, as untouched by the old Islamic civilisation that had conquered India as by the British; for 'kafir' in Arabic means 'unbeliever'. The scene is set for an exploit of mythical dimensions, and the feeling is further reinforced by references to Sarawak, the Pacific island ruled in despotic style by the family of the 'white rajah', Charles Brooke, and to the Indian Mutiny. 'This business', remarks Carnehan when the people turn against them, 'is our Fifty-Seven.' The history of the Empire, seen here as a series of magnificent adventures accompanied by inevitable disasters, is bound to repeat itself. The story celebrates the days of untrammelled imperial adventure, but is careful in the case of Dravot and Carnehan to use their ambiguous status as a means of balancing the mythical against the real. The memorable verisimilitude of the 'frame' which describes the journalist's encounter with the two loafers contrasts in itself with the less clearly visualised Kafiristan, but it also allows Kipling to hint at the unreality of his protagonists. When he first meets them they are plotting to pose as journalists in order to blackmail an Indian prince, and the narrator warns them that there is a real journalist on the scene; and when they set out on their expedition, 'I would have prayed for them, but that night a real king died in Europe and demanded an obituary notice.' The hint is broadened by the dreamlike way in which the two appear in the newspaper office, and by the mysterious disappearance of Dravot's crowned head at the end. In the British India of railway junctions where trains connect and offices where journalists grind away at their desks in the heat, they come and go like genii. Their redoubtable names (Daniel Dravot and Peachey Taliaferro Carnehan) and their manner of speaking give them a definite resemblance to the Elizabethan adventurers in Kipling's later romantic account of English history in *Puck of Pook's Hill*, and Dravot talks of being a knight of the Queen rather after the manner of Elizabeth I than Victoria. From their first appearance to Carnehan's wretched return they are simultaneously the most richly-coloured of romantic heroes and vagabonds doomed to their usual abysmal fate.

In Kafiristan the system of bureaucracy in which the Raj was enmeshed falls away, and Dravot rules by force of personality. He acts out a belief which goes as far back into colonial history as *Robinson Crusoe*; that white men may be transmuted into gods. Judging by this story it was a belief that still informed the determined moral rectitude of Anglo-Indian society. Dravot wilfully tears down his godhead by taking a native wife, and his mission is betrayed when she gives him a bite instead of a kiss, and the people of Kafiristan realise that ordinary blood flows in his veins. Kipling's heroes both celebrate the colonial myth and are used to keep it in perspective. He does not regard his adventurers as moral reprobates, but we are made aware that they do not in themselves represent imperial progress. The symbolic paper whirligigs that Dravot takes with him to trade when he leaves Lahore are repeated in his final fall from the rope bridge. In cutting his bridge and destroying him the natives of Kafiristan reject the bridge of civilisation across which, in Sir James Stephens' famous metaphor, such backward races were supposed to pass[21] but in two notable later stories, 'The Undertakers' (1896) and 'The Bridge Builders' (1898), Kipling makes symbolic use of bridges built from the steel which made mid-Victorian Britain economically supreme. In the romantic world of 'The Man Who Would Be King', however, the largeness and freedom that Mulvaney sometimes discovers are fully and flamboyantly realised. Although they are a throwback to a more swashbuckling and less stable past, and their tale is one of epic disaster, they partly anticipate the freshness with which Kim will explore the 'great and beautiful land' of British India itself.

In a rare comment on his own work in *Something of Myself* (7), Kipling commented that *Puck of Pook's Hill* 'had to be a balance to, as well as a seal upon, some aspects of my 'Imperialistic' output in the past.' It is a characteristically cryptic statement, but it seems reasonable to suppose that what he chiefly meant was that he had put India into a wider context. The 'English spirit', with its roots deep in the commingled influence of Viking, Roman, Norman and Saxon is celebrated in these children's stories, which thus provide a balance to, and a gracious apology for, his earlier impatience with the society to which he addressed the line 'And what do they know of England who only England know?' in 'The English Flag'. It is interesting to see that Kipling was consciously aware in this way of interconnections between his work. He speaks of the 'Puck' stories being written in layers, and in the stories that have been considered in this chapter there are also various patterns and a use of allusion – to Shakespeare, or nursery types, or various simple myths – which seem to be his way of asserting that, however topical the subject, his characters are also universal types. Our disgust with Georgie Porgie may be softened by the reflection that there have always been Georgie Porgies; Mulvaney is the archetypal 'rough diamond'; Dravot and Carnehan are loyal comrades. Of course all fiction uses such types, but Kipling has a particular knack of embellishing them by suddenly reminding us of Prometheus, or Antony and Cleopatra, or the heroes of the Mutiny. In *Puck of Pook's Hill* he sought relief from the present state of the Empire after the disillusionment of the Boer War, but he also furthered the strategy of having the heroes of history and legend step from the wings in response to the stage provided by the Empire. These earlier scattered allusions are symptoms of Kipling's own awareness that his fiction was tapping not just a new background in India but latent feelings and attitudes that had to be managed with care. His stories of working-class soldiers provided a vessel in which to blend heroic, moral and patriotic sentiments with the violence and sexual promise inherent in India.

4
Illustrating the Native Feature

The foolish person in search of a little disinterested information about things may find the so-called Indian Mutiny an unexplained historical phenomenon and eagerly hope for some enlightenment on the subject from a writer who is 'illustrating the native feature'. He will get little or none from Mr Kipling. . . . He will find the scantiest mention of or even allusion to the social movements of the natives.

So argued the radical poet Francis Adams in 1891.[1] In effect he combines two points here – that Kipling wilfully ignores Indian politics, as represented by the Indian journalism of Bombay and Calcutta, and by the newly-formed Indian Congress; and also that he sees Indians only in the mass, as 'raw, brown, naked humanity', as Kipling puts it in 'The Conversion of Aurelian McGoggin.'

The correctness of the first point is not at issue. Kipling had no time for the Indian's point of view, and his early journalism dismisses the political consciousness emerging in the big cities as an aberration. The second point involves critical judgement, although only a radical like Adams could have raised it in the nineties. Another distinguished early critic, Richard Le Gallienne, writes without irony of 'the romance of the English government in India.'[2] Since then the critical perspective has undoubtedly been changed by Kipling's most popular and sustained account of India in *Kim* (1901). Still, it is questionable whether Adams himself would have accepted that Kipling's treatment of 'natives' had fundamentally altered in this characteristic passage from Chapter 4 of *Kim*:

They met a troop of long-haired, strong-scented Sansis with baskets of lizards and other unclean food on their backs, the lean dogs sniffing at their heels. These people kept their own side of the road, moving at a quick, furtive jog-trot, and all other castes gave them ample room; for the Sansi is deep pollution. Behind them, walking wide and stiffly across the strong shadows, the memory of his leg-irons still on him, strode one newly released from jail; his full stomach and shiny skin to prove that the Government fed its prisoners better than most honest men could feed themselves. Kim knew that walk well, and made broad jest of it as they passed. Then an Akali, a wild-eyed, wild-haired Sikh devotee in the blue-checked clothes of his faith, with polished steel quoits glistening on the cone of his tall blue turban, stalked past, returning from a visit to one of the independent Sikh states, where he had been singing the glories of the Khalsa to college-trained princelings in top-boots and white cord breeches. Kim was careful not to irritate that man; for the Akali's temper is short and his arm is quick.

Descriptive moments like these have impressed several twentieth-century critics with the richness and diversity that Kipling in *Kim* finds in India. Yet despite the generosity of detail, and the obvious love of colour and movement that Kipling shares with us, he is still dealing here with India en masse, the Indian *crowd*. There is no doubting his affection for the *characteristic* moments of Indian life – in this respect his recording of Indian smells, and especially of Indian cooking, is even more impressive; but it falls short of entailing the respect of equals and the acceptance of the Indian as a real individual. Time and again Kipling draws Indian characters so deftly that they remain in the memory, but do so explicitly as *types*, so that the reader actually recalls them by means of a label: 'the Jat farmer' or 'the Amritsar courtesan'. As Arnold Kettle has pointed out, the two foreground figures who explore India in *Kim* – a British boy and a Tibetan lama – are *both* foreigners.[3]

One of the delightful things about Kim himself is that his education appears to consist of a series of holidays. We are seduced by his whole-hearted approach to India, but it must not be forgotten that India is so enjoyable precisely because it is all at his disposal. Although Kim learns a great deal, he does not have to unlearn this attitude in order to take on adult responsibilities when he goes to work for the government. He is perfectly suited by his 'native' background to the education that Kipling designs for him; for if India is still a foreign land in *Kim*, there is a new emphasis on the need for its rulers to know and respect it – in much the same way, one might say, as an educated gentleman in the nineteenth century had to know Italy or France. We find, for example, some vehement criticism of one British attitude typical of lower-class white men. Of the drummer-boy who is temporarily put in charge of Kim we are told that 'He did not care for any of the bazars that were within bounds. He styled all natives "niggers"; yet servants and sweepers called him abominable names to his face, and, misled by their deferential attitude, he never understood.' (6). To some Anglo-Indians, at least, this must have been a vaguely alarming comment. The 'real' sahibs, however, are in an altogether different case. All are, indeed, experts on Indian languages and customs. Such a sahib is Creighton, the spymaster who recruits Kim to the service: 'No man could be a fool who knew the language so intimately, who moved so gently and silently, and whose eyes were so different from the dull fat eyes of other sahibs.' (7) Among such men ignorance is a cardinal sin. Creighton explicitly warns Kim that recruits who 'contemn the black man' and 'feign not to understand him' have their pay cut for ignorance (7).

The extent to which Kipling is willing to modify traditional British prejudice and isolationism is reflected in the school to which Kim is sent, which is Catholic and mainly attended by the children of well-to-do Eurasian parents. These boys have the advantage of knowing India far more intimately than the upper echelons of the 'pure' English who stay within their cantonments. Nevertheless, 'When tales were told of hot nights, Kim did not sweep the board with reminiscences; for St Xavier's looks down on boys who "go native" altogether. One must never forget that one is a Sahib, and that some day, when examinations are passed, one will command natives.'(8) In his account of the school Kipling thus gives his seal of approval to the Eurasian establishment. We should be reminded here of the 'second fighting-line of Eurasians' that he envisages in 'His Private Honour'. Clearly such approval has to be treated with caution, for the racism of Kipling's day, as indeed of our own, is not always so clear-cut as to be instantly identifiable, but comprises a system that makes numerous distinctions. Kipling may accept the Eurasians who attend public school and are destined for careers in medicine, law, or administration as sahibs, but not the signaller Michele D'Cruz in 'His Chance in Life', who has only one drop of white blood in him. Nor will he necessarily allow that miscegenation is ever really desirable. Race, class, and caste tend to overlap to create distinctions, but 'racial purity' remains fairly fundamental. It

1. *Punch* on the Russian threat to the Raj.

2. An obscure heroine of the Raj.

3. The evils of the caste-system, according to *Punch*.

4. An interesting depiction of a dispute between empires.

THE BURMESE TOAD.

5. King Theebaw's deposition by the British. France, the imperial rival, is reflected in the water.

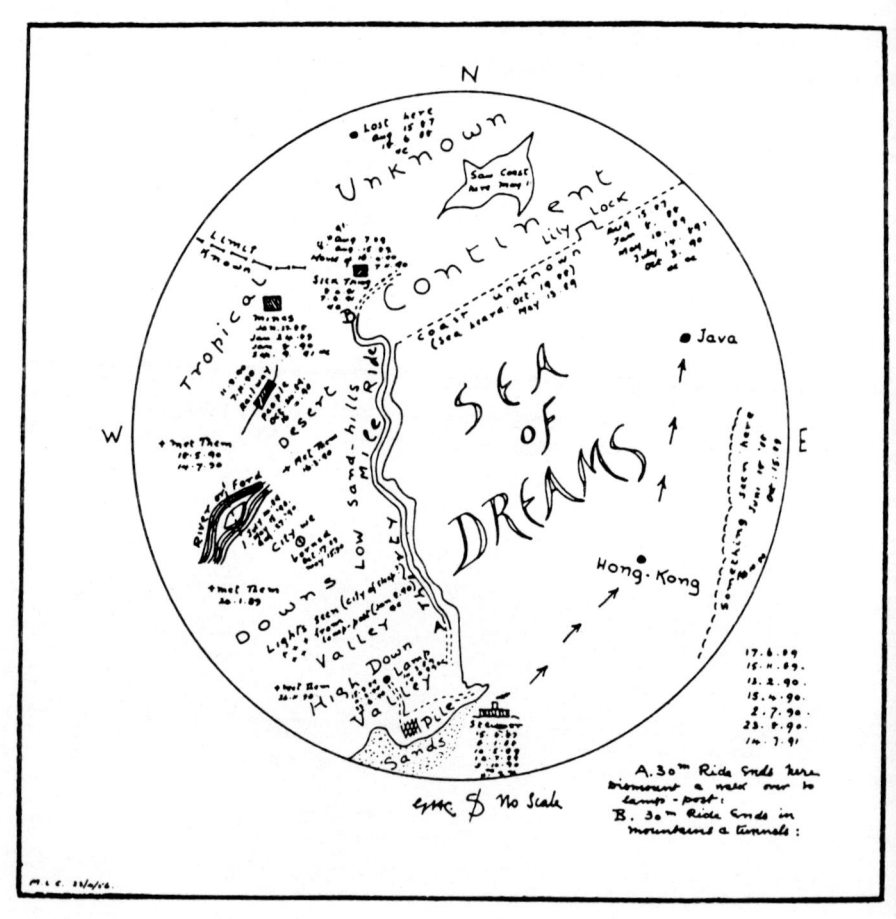

6. Kipling's ever-practical imperialist even practises cartography in his dreams.

7. An ingenuous view of Kipling, the seer of British India.

8. One of Beerbohm's stinging caricatures with the caption 'Mr Rudyard Kipling takes a bloomin' day aht on the blasted 'eath, with Britannia, 'is gurl'.

may seem odd that in the first draft of *Kim* one of Kim's adversaries is described by Kipling as a 'nigger', but the criticism levelled at the drummer-boy in the published version is that he does not *distinguish* between 'niggers' – Holderness's 'Dravidians' and 'coolies' – and other Indian races.[4] Again, in the published version, the Afghan Mahbub Ali nearly stabs Kim because he calls him 'Kala Admi' – a black man – but refrains upon remembering that Kim, although he looks like a native, is a pure white sahib. What is true is not that Kipling has become non-racist in outlook, but that his attention is on the 'better' representatives of various racial groups: those whom he imagines may work in harmony with the British government, rather than those who pose a nuisance or a threat. But if Kipling's racism has altered only by degrees, there is a wholesale change in his imaginative assimilation of India. Throughout his career, since, for example, 'The Story of Muhammed Din', Kipling had often written about particular Indians with affection and respect. In Lahore he had belonged to a freemason's lodge that included representatives of almost every race in India. In all this work, however, racial characteristics are quite unalterable, and the British are inevitably 'superior' in the long run. In *Kim* the British retain their superiority, but for the first time they have something to learn from the 'simple, tolerant folk' of India. In the preface to *Life's Handicap* Kipling finely remarks that 'when man has come to the turnstiles of Night all the creeds in the world seem to him wonderfully alike and colourless'. There is an abundance of colour and of different customs in *Kim*, and its impact is such that Kipling is doing more than observing and celebrating the difference. There is at least scope for a more complex characterisation of members of other races; a sense that they may also change and develop with experience. The relationship of Kim with the lama is at the heart of this shift in attitude, but it shows itself in small things as well as large ones. When the detective Strickland first dons native disguise in 'Miss Youghal's Sais' (1888) he is unable to stomach native tobacco, but Kim smokes it for preference.

It is nevertheless the white men who hold all the threads of the 'Great Game' of espionage which in Kim's phrase, 'runs like a shuttle through all Hind'. The expression 'Great Game' originated in the context of the First Afghan war of 1839, and then became current as a description of British Eastern diplomacy in general, so that its use in *Kim* relocates it and indirectly asserts the political primacy of India and its north-west frontier. The actual system of espionage described in *Kim* is based on fact, down to the terminology of 'players' and 'games', and the use of a wooden rosary to count the paces in clandestine survey work. Though they are trustworthy 'players', Kipling's agents are controlled from a centre which processes their information.⁵

Among his native friends Kim is the 'Friend of all the World' and 'Friend of the Stars', and the India he finds is there, like these enjoyably Oriental appellations, to be enjoyed and savoured. It is appropriate to such enjoyment that the book should have an episodic feel. In his autobiography Kipling described it as 'nakedly picaresque' and cited Cervantes. The allusion is fitting in the other sense that the India traversed by Kim and the lama is a peasant society; much of the colour and good humour with which it is described is made possible by the endearing simplicity of its inhabitants, who become progressively more simple as the story moves into the mountainous regions near Nepal and Tibet. Kipling's account of his inability to 'make a plot' is somewhat disingenuous, for the book is tightly organised around a clear double structure.⁶ Kim and the lama undertake two journeys together, each of which ends in a discovery. In the middle there is a hiatus covering the time that Kim spends at school. The first part of the novel leads to the discovery that Kim is a sahib; the second is concerned with discovering what it means to be a sahib. In typically Victorian fashion the discovery of a new identity involves a need to be educated into new social norms, and this is what the hiatus between journeys stresses. The fascinating jewel-dealer Lurgan who trains Kim in espionage skills is in the end a superior kind of schoolmaster: ' "By Jove! O'Hara, I think there is a great deal in you; but you must not become proud and you must not talk." ' (9). It is only when the new lessons have been sufficiently rubbed in that Kim can set out with the lama again, but bearing this time not only his cheerful ability to blend in with Indian life but also his formal qualifications in espionage work and, most importantly, his sahib's mentality. Kim is now on equal terms with his fellow-agent, Mahbub Ali, whose pawn and messenger he has been. The pleasant paradox of *Kim* is that his burgeoning sahibdom brings him closer to his people, the Indians themselves.

'And who are thy people, Friend of all the World?'
'This great and beautiful land', said Kim, waving his paw round the little clay-walled room where the oil-lamp in its niche

burned heavily through the tobacco-smoke. 'And, further, I would see my Lama again. And further, I need money.' (8)

This statement to Mahbub is important, signalling that Kim is destined to become not merely one of the better type of sahibs, but a sahib of a virtually new type; one with a real and deep affection for India. The affectionate irony with which 'this great and beautiful land' is contrasted with the smoky interior is a reinforcing measure; India as we have seen it through Kim's eyes *is* beautiful. Sahib though he is, Kim also needs the lama, and it is through serving as his disciple that he finds fulfilment and is integrated with his people. For although the lama is not of India, he represents the spirit of India. In one of the most assured passages in the book the lama's wanderings while Kim is at school are sketched in, and he is described 'coming and going across India as softly as a bat'. (9) Bat-like movement, flitting, responding to echoes, could well serve as an image for the people of India in *Kim*. It contrasts with the symbol of benevolent British domination, the railways, whose presence is constantly felt in the book. 'The government has brought on us many taxes', observes a farmer from the Punjab, 'but it gives us one good thing – the *te-rain* that joins friends and unites the anxious. A wonderful matter is the *te-rain*.' (11) Kipling's style subtly reflects the contrast between the indirections and the relaxed quality of the Indian way of life and the ordered world of the British. 'They entered the fort-like railway station, black in the end of night; the electrics sizzling over the goods-yard where they handle the heavy northern grain-traffic.' (2) The same elegant balancing of clauses and use of assonance is employed to create the 'Indian' quality of the Jain temple at Benares:

> The Oswal, at peace with mankind, carried the message into the darkness behind him, and the easy, uncounted Eastern minutes slid by; for the lama was asleep in his cell, and no priest would wake him. When the click of his rosary again broke the hush of the inner court where the calm images of the Arhats stand, a novice whispered, 'Thy *chela* is here', and the old man strode forth, forgetting the end of that prayer. (11)

It is very important that Kipling seeks, through his prose, to portray in *Kim* an India that has its own inward movement and rhythm. Kipling described his method of literary composition in *Something of Myself*, in which he progressively deleted from his first draft until he was left with what was essential. It is a method that has been deprecated as well as praised, on the grounds that what the resulting style gains in vigour and compression is lost in possible ambiguity, and that the net result is too inflexible an instrument.[7] In *Kim*, too, Kipling's passion for figures with sharply etched outlines, and for the *mot juste*, impose limitations on the India he portrays, as in this description:

> Then they met Sikander Khan coming down with a few unsaleable screws – remnants of his string – and Mahbub, who has more of horse-coping in his little finger-nail than Sikander Khan in all his tents, must needs buy two of the worst, and that meant eight hours of laborious diplomacy and untold tobacco. (8)

This, too, is elegant; but here it is impossible not to be aware of the narrator's voice and its controlling power – as, for example, in the faintly ironic 'laborious diplomacy and untold tobacco'. The ways of Muslim horse-dealers are, one feels here, fixed to all eternity. The Indian scene that emerges is at times too predictable, and too plastically subservient to Kipling the craftsman and Kipling the imperialist. Mahbub Ali is, indeed, the wily and ferocious type of Pathan that we meet throughout Kipling's work. If we see only his virtues in *Kim* this does not mean that he ever steps beyond the cocoon of racial characteristics, into which his paternal feelings for Kim neatly fit. Both he and Kim's other secret service mentor Hurree Chunder Mookerjee are 'supermen' to some extent. Thus Mahbub is shown restraining his *native* instinct for bloodletting in order better to conceal his identity, just as Hurree is shown overcoming his *native* timidity when his work as an agent demands it. 'Watch him', Kipling exhorts us, 'all babudom laid aside'. (15) It is only the super-spy who can doff, but not alter, his racial type; but Hurree is also as much an old Roman as a Bengali: 'Rolled in the Babu, robed as to the shoulders like a Roman emperor, jowled like Titus' (15) – an impression which Lockwood Kipling's original illustration strongly confirms.[8]

It is only through the lama that we sense an India freed from preordained characteristics and able to develop independently. He represents a simplicity that, convenient though it may be to Kipling, seems to go deeper than typecasting. It is at the point in the book where the lama, laden with his spiritual difficulties, returns to the simple life of the mountains that we come across a scene that Edmund Wilson rightly described as unmatched in Kipling.[9]

> Then they thawed out in the sun, and sat with their legs hanging over infinite abysses, chattering, laughing, and smoking. They judged India and its government solely from their experience of wandering Sahibs who had employed them or their friends as shikarris. Kim heard tales of shots missed upon ibex, serow, or markhor, by Sahibs twenty years in their graves – every detail lighted from behind like twigs on tree-tops seen against lightning. (14)

Whatever its weakness, Kipling's sharp, unambiguous style – unconsciously imaged for us here in the simile of the twigs – renders convincingly this basic sense of uncomplicated human community. Descriptive passages like this, and the portrayal of the lama in the Jain temple illuminate Nirad C. Chaudhuri's remark that Kipling 'stands supreme among Western writers for his treatment of the biggest reality in India, which is made up of the life of people and religion in the twin setting of the mountains and the plains.'[10] Against this setting the sign that the lama discovers in his torn chart can be presented as valid on its own terms: 'Kim stared at the brutally disfigured chart. From left to right diagonally the rent ran – from the Eleventh House where Desire gives birth to the Child (as it is drawn by Tibetans) – across the human and animal worlds, to the Fifth House – the empty House of the Senses. The logic was unanswerable.' (14) We are not expected to take this literally, but it would obviously be a grave mistake to dismiss it as 'native superstition'; a mistake which is in fact made by the Russian spies who are the tokenistic villains of *Kim*. The same is true of the lama's final 'discovery' of his sacred river after his final meditation. While we do not literally believe in the river, as Kim himself clearly does not, we recognise a spiritual state which has, above all, contributed to Kim's education.

> About the end of the first century B.C. there was something of a split in the ranks (of Buddhism) resulting from an attempt to restore it to a popular basis. This led to the evolution of the Boddhisattvas, beings who on the threshold of Nirvana set aside their entry into the final state of bliss and remained in the sinful world out of compassion for others to whose salvation they became devoted. . . . Whatever the merits of this development it

inevitably led to the growth of myths attendant on the peculiar virtues of each one of them. The way was open to a compromise with Hindu teachings.[11]

There is clearly a possible analogy between the action of the Bodhisattvas and the sacrifice of Christ, and it is noticeable that in *Kim* the Bodhisat is always mentioned as a single individual, as he is in Kipling's poem 'The Buddha at Kamakura' (1892). In those verses the Christian pantheon seems to influence Kipling further, as the single Bodhisat is amalgamated with the father-figure of the Buddha. It is certainly the action of the Boddhisattvas that the lama imitates in his own mind at the end of *Kim*. His account is counterpointed by the commonsense view of the other characters, who see an old man tumbling into a brook and having to be fished out; yet the comicality of the lama never really diminishes respect for his special qualities. At the last, Kim 'peered at the cross-legged figure, outlined in jet-black against the lemon-coloured drift of the light. So does the stone Bodhisat sit who looks down upon the patent self-registering turnstiles of the Lahore Museum.' (15) With this the entire novel wheels back to its opening scene, and it does so with some intent, for the museum is presided over by the kindly curator (whose resemblance to John Lockwood – Kipling the father – was recognisable even at the time of publication) who serves the lama as the model of the kind of sahib he would like Kim to become. As Edmund Wilson has pointed out, Kim is clearly destined to be rather more of a soldier than a scholar.[12] The argument, however, that Kim's career as a spy is a 'betrayal' of the Indian people is misconceived. The Indians of *Kim* are not looking for independence, and nothing about the Indian world that Kipling depicts contradicts the notion that spying is an honourable service to them. It matters that Kim's own question, 'What is Kim?' changes to 'Who is Kim?' – that the affectionate mood of the novel is geared to a vision of India in which sahibs and natives no longer occupy entrenched positions. But such a vision presupposes that the Indians are willing subordinates to the British. The remark of one of the Russians that 'It is *we* who can deal with the Orientals' is exposed as fatuous, but the underlying implication is that if British were substituted for Russian, then the remark might embody truth.

Every aspect of *Kim* reveals its purpose as a blueprint for India as a country under permanent and beneficient British rule. The gentle ways of the lama complement rather than challenge this conception. Yet although the figure that Kim sees outlined in jet black is akin to the final piece in the colourful jig-saw puzzle India that Kipling has constructed, he emerges with a rare degree of individuality. The two journeys through which Kim finds his place in the world are also learning experiences for the already wise lama. There is a mystery behind his very simplicity, and the story of Kim's growth to adulthood is finally of less interest than the shadows he casts. As Kim's mentor, the lama is joined by the 'Sahiba', the rich widow and grandmother who presides over the final unity. She stands, in the scheme of *Kim*, for India on its benevolent physical, rather than spiritual side. Like Kim and the lama, she too is seeing India on a jaunt, for it is a curious fact that the thronging, colourful world of *Kim* does not in the end contain any real account of Indian people engaged in their ordinary working lives. With the Sahiba we encounter a manner of describing India that is familiar from Kipling's earlier work: 'The patterns on the gold-worked curtains ran up and down, melting and re-forming as the folds shook and quivered to the night wind; and when the talk grew more earnest the jewelled forefinger snapped out little sparks of light between the embroideries.' (4) This takes us back to Mulvaney's description of the princesses in 'The Incarnation of Krishna Mulvaney', or to the jewel-hoard in 'The King's Ankus', which Angus Wilson has aptly described as written in a 'restrained Yellow-Book manner'.[13] The Orient stirs seductively for a moment in the description of the Sahiba's conveyance, but in the very few such moments when the sensuous hints at the sensual, Kim's magic charm is such that they bring him pure relief: 'Kneaded to irresponsible pulp, half hypnotised by the perpetual flick and readjustment of the uneasy *chudders* that veiled their eyes, Kim slid ten thousand miles into slumber'. (15)

In the end the tolerant, celebratory mood of *Kim* is surely both a gain and a loss. The tension beneath the surface of his early work, caused by a real struggle to mould at least some of the actualities of civilian and army life into an acceptable yet desirable picture of India has gone. The 'evil presence' of those early stories is still officially supposed to exist in *Kim*, but it is reduced to meaninglessness by the pronouncement that the boy Kim 'had known all evil since he could speak'. In reality Kim is always too much the almost disembodied Puck figure, the 'Friend of the Stars', for the process of his growth to be made interesting. His fulfilment ·is to realise that he is simply part of the everyday world: 'Roads were meant to be walked upon, houses to be lived in, cattle to be driven, fields to be tilled, and men and women to be talked to.' (15).

Kipling seems to have ignored the fact that one cannot make a *bildungsroman* out of such a plain tale. But although *Kim* is a blueprint that produces an arbitrary resolution of the conflict between India and the British, it produces an 'India' which is more than the result of sheer manipulation. The unexpectedness of the lama's interventions in particular give it, within the obvious limits that Kipling imposes, an independent life. It is through the lama, too, that Kim himself acquires a vitality rare among the heroes of what the book essentially is: Victorian boys' fiction – 'I have known many men in my so long life, and disciples not a few. But to none among men, if so be thou are woman-born, has my heart gone out as it has to thee – thoughtful, wise, and courteous, but something of a small imp.' (4)

Undoubtedly, the works that Kipling wrote primarily for a young audience are his most rounded, and those in which a sense of achievement is felt most strongly. In those stories where he deals with entirely 'adult' themes and emotions – from 'On Greenhow Hill' and 'Love-o'-Women' to 'The Wish House' and 'Friendly Brook' – he produced haunting, entirely convincing, but fragmentary portrayals of grief, jealousy and despair. It is hardly surprising that at neither stage in his career could he sustain work on this level through a volume of stories. His one truly 'adult' novel, *The Light that Failed*, is hopelessly lacking in poise between its few memorable scenes. Happy as he was with the minutiae of prose composition, Kipling obviously found the quality of completeness hard to come by. 'Did you stop, or did it?' asked his discerning father of *Kim*; and on being told that the answer was 'it', remarked 'Then it oughtn't to be too bad.'[14] In *Kim*, but also in works as diverse in their construction as the two *Jungle Books*, the *Just-So Stories*, *Puck of Pook's Hill* and *Rewards and Fairies*, one senses that Kipling has said what he wants to say and found the requisite pattern. Although few would regard *Captains Courageous* and *Stalky & Co.* as on quite the same level, Kipling again seems equable in his treatment of each episode, secure in his purposes. In all these works there is an almost hypnotic quality about the locale. Paradigmatic is the 'great grey-green, greasy Limpopo River, all set about with fever trees' that is the Elephant's Child's destination in *Just-So Stories*, but from this hyper-tropical description to the paraphernalia of Study Number Five, all betray the story-teller's pleasure in itemising a scene. In each of these works there is also an openly pedagogic element, but with it goes an absence of pressure and tension, a lightness of tone. The exempla are there, but they are made pleasant by a more 'unbuttoned' Kipling who is eager to explore these imaginary worlds with his young audience.

Pedagogy and sense of enchantment are both powerfully present in the *Jungle Books*, the earliest of this group. The setting is not the Anglo-India of his earlier tales, but the remote Seeonee Jungle which Kipling knew only from the descriptions and photographs of his Allahabad friends the Hills.[15] The jungle that Kipling creates for Mowgli is a curious amalgam. It is a place to be explored with the relish of childhood, and yet an evocation of a stereotypical 'India' of dark luxuriance and hidden danger. In *The Jungle Book* (1894) and *The Second Jungle Book* (1896) we can observe, clinging to the lessons that are absorbed, the dark and treacherous side of 'India' that is only finally dispensed with in *Kim*. Outside the 'Mowgli' stories themselves, it is most noticeable in the gruesome animal story 'The Undertakers', the only work in which Kipling comments directly on the 'Indian Mutiny' of 1857. A more benign parable is provided in 'Rikki Tikki Tavi', the story of the adopted mongoose who loyally fights off the cobras which threaten the English family in their bungalow. The balance that has to be struck here is between the white liberal's refusal to look death in the face, and the mongoose's (i.e. loyal native's) utterly casual acceptance of it. 'The Miracle of Purun Bhagat', by contrast, shares its affectionate and relaxed tone with *Kim*. The knighted Indian Prime Minister who takes up a begging bowl and becomes a pilgrim (a 'sannyasi' as laid down by Hindu custom) is an idealised subject, in whom, significantly, the man of action comes finally to the fore as he emerges from his cell to warn the villagers of a landslip. Perhaps we scarcely need to be told that when he is moved along by a policeman in Simla, 'Purun Bhagat salaamed reverently to the Law, because he knew the value of it, and was seeking for a Law of his own.'

These assorted fables are interesting and, of course, highly polished; but they are peripheral to the more complex series of stories about Mowgli which form the core of both volumes. The story of Mowgli's growth to manhood has obvious parallels with *Kim*, but the jungle world is less benevolent and, paradoxically in view of its fabulistic element, less neatly arranged. The difference in emphasis is most apparent in the fact that when the Mowgli stories are considered as a whole it immediately strikes us that Mowgli does *not* belong to the jungle. Throughout the eight stories the saying that 'man returns to man at last' runs like a motif, and considerable space is given to the pain that this tactlessly uttered wisdom causes Mowgli, and to his sense of betrayal by the jungle community, even among those who are his closest allies. Mowgli is undoubtedly the young 'sahib' of the jungle, and he has to contend with the 'native ingratitude' that his superiority arouses: ' "The others they hate thee because their eyes cannot meet thine; because thou art wise; because thou hast pulled out thorns from their feet – because thou art a man." ' The point of the allegory, however, is not merely to confirm that sense of ingratitude, but to give it a depth that the Anglo-Indian's aloof stance would not normally permit. Mowgli, by contrast, 'was furious with rage and sorrow, for, wolf-like, the wolves had never told him how they hated him.'[16] The final story, 'The Spring Running' (in *The Second Jungle Book*), resolves the issue finally, as Mowgli chooses to return to mankind, but it also probes more deeply the experience of the white man who may feel excluded from the life around him. This is strikingly – and classically, in terms of the white man's latent response to India – expressed in an 'aside' in 'The Spring Running':

> A girl in a white cloth came down some path that led from the outskirts of the village. Gray Brother dropped out of sight at once, and Mowgli backed noiselessly into a field of high-springing crops. He could almost have touched her with his hand when the warm, green stalks closed before his face and he disappeared like a ghost. The girl screamed, for she thought she had seen a spirit, and then she gave a deep sigh. Mowgli parted the stalks with his hands and watched her till she was out of sight.

This is quite a startling passage to find in what is, after all, a late-Victorian collection of stories for children. It serves to underline the depth of Kipling's preoccupation with feelings and problems that we have seen him explore under the aegis of his soldier stories. The net result of Mowgli's astonishing strength and beauty is that he nas no natural home or community. The sahib in India suffers the loneliness of a god among mere mortals.

This is one aspect of the *Jungle Books* that has been completely submerged in the history of its reception, especially in the wider sense of its imitations, its adoption by the Scout Movement, and its transmogrification by Walt Disney. It is interesting to find Kipling turning aside in his autobiography to make this delicately barbed comment about imitators:

My *Jungle Books* begat zoos of them. But the genius of the genii was the one who wrote a series called *Tarzan of the Apes*. . . . He had 'jazzed' the motif of the *Jungle Books* and, I imagine, he had thoroughly enjoyed himself. He was reported to have said that he wanted to find out how bad a book he could write and 'get away with it', which is a legitimate ambition. (8)

Thus Kipling himself seems to have seen the qualities of his work drowning in the welter of its own popularity. Consistent with this is the surprise with which we discover that in the original Mowgli always feels out of place in his jungle. Life in the jungle has a depth and richness through the addition of this painful edge to the tremendous verve with which it is described, and the variety of pedagogical trails laid in it; for as fable these stories read rather like *Paradise Lost, Gulliver's Travels* and *Emile* rolled into one.

In one respect the jungle is a kind of ideal public school, where Mowgli 'grew and grew strong as a boy must who does not know that he is learning any lessons, and who has nothing in the world to think of except things to eat.'[17] This apparently cavalier attitude towards more formal methods of learning is certainly related to the ethos of many British public schools, and with it goes the existence of a set of elaborate 'jungle laws' which lay down precisely what one should and should not do, rules which are sanctioned by tradition and to be learned by rote. It is this version of *The Jungle Book*, not forgetting the pedagogue Baloo and the 'school bully' Shere Khan, which is still handed down today.

In 'Kaa's Hunting' there is an unmistakable similarity between the Bandar-Log who kidnap Mowgli and the Yahoos of *Gulliver's Travels*. Both are species of monkeys, and therefore stand for men, and both are portrayed as idle and senseless because they lack any organisation or any code of social conduct. As a satire on democracy, Kipling's story is both less caustic and less ambivalent than Swift's, for the line of satire does not waver as it does with Swift, between ideas of democracy and of humanity as a whole. There is no danger of Mowgli's perceiving himself as Bandar-Log, although the comparison is readily applied in another story to the native villagers that he encounters.

As if to make up for the bluntness of the messages they transmit in this way, the *Jungle Books* produce a further proliferation of them. In 'How Fear Came' it is implied that the jungle world is in a fallen state, from which the rigid heirarchies of 'caste', the division into

Eaters of Grass and Eaters of Flesh, and so on, has evolved. 'The King's Ankus', on the other hand, is a reworking of another ancient theme, in which the jungle is innocent of the evil brought about by acquisition, with Mowgli as its 'noble savage'. 'Tiger, Tiger' narrates the uninhibited revenge that Mowgli takes on Shere Khan, but it too points a moral – the tiger is destroyed by his own sloth and arrogance. 'Red Dog' returns to the theme of the aristocratic few standing out against the mob. One cannot miss the resemblance between the battle of the wolves against the red dogs and Kipling's other great set-piece description of battle, the stand of the British square against the dervishes in *The Light That Failed*.

This plethora of lessons is kept buoyant by Kipling's powers of dramatic narration, and by the delight he takes in his animals, like 'Bagheera, the Black Panther, inky black all over, but with the panther markings showing up in certain lights like the pattern of watered silk.'[18] Kipling's diction conveys both a sense of grandeur and a sense of fun. When required, as in 'Letting In the Jungle', descriptions are exaggerated in mock-epic style: 'Mowgli threw out his hand, and as Hathi (the elephant) wheeled the moonlight showed a long white scar on his slaty side, as though he had been struck with a red-hot whip.' Yet the jungle remains remarkably lifelike, and a number of contemporary reviews express a sense of puzzlement that Kipling can write as 'accurately' of this animal kingdom as he can of natives or of British soldiers. Their alignment of the *Jungle Books* with Kipling's earlier Indian fiction is not altogether naive, for the Mowgli stories do compound two kinds of remoteness; the remoteness engendered by the mannerisms of the narrator and the reworking of ancient themes, and the actual physical remoteness of the Seeonee jungle from the English reader. The descriptions of the native village and its inhabitants have the important function of insisting that the jungle is not entirely mythical, since the village itself is clearly not. It is precisely this compound scenario that gives resonance to the production of some of the tropes of 'latent orientalism'.

All of the stories have their own logic, and this is not meant to suggest that Kipling's preoccupation with the state of the Raj mars their other qualities. The Indian villagers do, however, belong to an 'India' that is familiar to us. They are childishly superstitious and easily transformed into a vindictive mob. At one moment the jungle is a world outside everyday reality, representing an 'India' that entered into its fallen state aeons ago. At other times the jungle is only physically remote from the present, and somewhere just beyond Mowgli's ken there is an English outpost where they 'govern all the land and do not suffer people to burn or beat each other without witnesses.'[19] There is more to this mixture of levels than blithe indifference on Kipling's part. Within this setting, images that convey a specifically 'oriental' danger and darkness are deftly superimposed on the narrative: 'The light of the torches streamed into the room where, stretched at full length on the bed, his paws crossed and lightly hung down over one end, black as the Pit, and terrible as a demon, was Bagheera.'[20] Real panther and symbolic role are locked together, just as the dance with which Kaa the python mesmerises the Bandar-Log is both convincing natural history and an image of India's dire fascination; as are the 'dark, oily streaks' floating from the tiger's chin when he drinks after he has killed a man. In the nature of things the jungle cannot be the pacified, civilised India that we mostly find in *Kim*. The *Jungle Books* in fact contain much of the note of apprehensiveness to be found in the early stories. While the figure of Mowgli points forward to *Kim*, the *Jungle Books* as a whole look to inculcate in their young readership not only the public-school virtues, but a warning of the danger and isolation to be met with in India.

The project of making India 'truly British' was one in which, in general, the British never seriously believed. The imposition of a western infrastructure of administration, education, judiciary and transport systems under the Raj took place alongside a basic conviction that Indians would never in fact assimilate Western culture, the 'superiority' of which seemed obvious to almost every British observer. Against this pessimism Kipling projects, from 'His Private Honour' through to *Kim*, an idea of greater British involvement with India, leading to a new kind of 'sahib' who feels at home in India and understands its customs, while remaining a member of an all-white ruling caste. The allegory of the *Jungle Books* seems to call into question this hopeful vision. In spite of the fact that most of the jungle animals prove to be loyal friends and servants to the 'sahib' Mowgli, he has no power to change them, and is forced in the end to depart. The Mowgli stories, however, are more than the sum of their curious mixture of elements. The feelings with which we are familiar from the experiences of Kipling's Anglo-Indians are one aspect of the stories; quite another is the awareness that, beyond their rather specious comradeship, Mowgli and his fellows are engaged in a common struggle for survival. It is the clear knowledge that the wolves' entire pattern of existence is at stake that gives depth to the furious excitement of 'Red Dog'; the acute understanding that their economy is balanced on a knife-edge that gives poignancy to the justifiable retribution that Mowgli sends the villagers in 'Letting In the Jungle'. The harshness of the natural world is always to be felt beneath the high colouring of Kipling's descriptions because it is understood as part of a process. Even Shere Khan's individual evil and cowardice are set firmly in this context. The exceptional circumstances in which he may kill mankind and drink beside the deer are used to increase our awareness of the basic ecological pattern. Greatly to its advantage, Kipling's imaginary world is in tune with the ideas of Darwin.

A major effect of the theory of evolution, certainly reflected in the writing of George Eliot and Thomas Hardy, was to unsettle the Victorian confidence in all kinds of 'progress'. If civilisation was the latest stage not of conscious human endeavour so much as of the struggle for survival, there could be far less certainty that progress as a whole was universally beneficial, and 'civilisation' itself could not be comfortably taken as the conquest of a mere animal existence if it might be no more than a development from it. The question that presents itself in Kipling's case is how far his emphasis on discipline and law in society simply ignores the background of struggle thrown up by Darwin's theory, and how far it is a reaction to it. In her *Darwin's Plots* Gillian Beer mentions Kipling's *Just-So Stories* as a throwback to Lamarck's theory of evolution rather than Darwin's. Just as Lamarck had suggested that some birds acquired long legs as a result of deliberately stretching them in order not to get their plumage wet, so Kipling uses intentionality to explain how the camel got his hump and the rhinoceros his skin, as well as how the tiger got his stripes in 'How Fear Came'.[21] Obviously this can be seen as entirely natural in the context of writing for children, but there is a further point, which is that in Kipling's stories the causal explanations are stretched to the point of absurdity. Where Lamarck's aim is coherence and plausibility, Kipling's primary aim is not really explanation at all. The sailor who makes a grating for the whale's throat is primarily a humorous example of what Kipling called 'stalkiness': a resourceful combination of determination, wit, and low cunning, designed chiefly for the benefit of heathen adversaries on the North-West Frontier. This whimsical pretence at casual explanation has proved popular in childrens' fiction ever since, but it may also suggest a deeper awareness that man's stalkiness, like Dravot's bluff, is a fragile resource in a hostile environment. The magical world that Kipling creates for children makes a virtue of the slightly overstrained vitality that Kim and Mulvaney have in common. Several critics have detected a fundamental pessimism or stoicism in Kipling's work, but if he has a philosophy it never frees itself entirely from his experience of India, and he fluctuates between a realisation of the struggle inherent in life itself and resentment at the hardships suffered by his own chosen breed. The element of fantasy in works like the *Jungle Books* is favourable to the former, but there is always a risk that exploration will give way to escapism. In *The Naulakha*, for example, the native state of 'Gokral Seetarun' – many of whose details are drawn from the same first-hand experience as *Letters of Marque* – is allowed to take on the extravagances of Rider Haggard's Africa: a place in which we should not be surprised to find breast-shaped mountains and thousand-year-old monarchs.

In many British minds, of course, India was by definition a land in which the impossible was known to happen; indeed few popular novels set in India at the time could be considered complete without a scene in which one of the native characters defies temporal or gravitational laws. Lurgan in *Kim* knows one or two such tricks, but they are only tricks. On the whole Kipling avoids the Indian juggler or fakir, though there is an unpleasant piece of sorcery in 'The Mark of the Beast'. Much more important to Kipling is the escape that the 'native' world may offer to his readers from their own social customs. I have suggested that the fantastic setting of the *Jungle Books* creates an opportunity for deeper reflection. The element of fantasy is not so apparent in 'Without Benefit of Clergy', in which the harshness of nature takes the form of a city stricken by cholera. It is, however, by achieving a similar degree of distance in his portrayal of a purely Indian ménage that Kipling in this story penetrates the starchiness and deliberately cultivated ignorance of a section of the Anglo-Indian community. That community is not openly criticised as it is at times in *Kim*, but it is found wanting, and so too is any over-casual association of India with the exotic and the erotic. In 'Without Benefit of Clergy' the extended description of a white man's native household creates a charmed circle quite unlike the furtive encounter of the earlier 'Beyond the Pale'. It is the fact that here we have *the* archetypal Victorian scenario – the scene of domestic bliss – that reveals both the sense of exploration of real dilemmas and the element of fantasy involved.

Whereas a common difficulty for English bachelors at home was having to endure years of waiting before they could enter into matrimony, Holden simply purchases his bride, Ameera, and immediately assumes the role of husband. In his house in the city, 'his feet could only pass beyond the outer courtyard to the women's rooms; and when the big wooden gate was bolted behind him he was king in his own territory, with Ameera for queen.' This is one of the remarkable stories that Kipling wrote during his own period of bachelorhood in London, when he was also reflecting in greater depth on his experience of Anglo-India. Bachelorhood in London, as we discover in the work of Gissing and James, as well as in Kipling's own novel, *The Light That Failed*, could be a lonely and miserable affair. Flourishing prostitution was the compensation offered by society, but rigidly abhorred by Kipling, a caste-conscious outsider who marvels at the impropriety of using white women as servants, and who writes with coy indignation that he suspects his aunt's maid of trying to seduce him.[22]

Although an exotic world of Muslim sacrifices, red-lacquered couches, flat roofs and silver bracelets is present everywhere in the story, it is no longer an India that the white man both fears and desires. Rather, it is absorbed into a double-sided dream that encompasses domestic bliss and Oriental passion. There is no tension here between the relationship of individuals and the wider relationship proposed between India and the British, and the story's tragic outcome is by no means the equivalent of the open warning against racial mixes in 'Beyond the Pale'. The Anglo-Indian world, when it is present at all, is used to heighten the tension building up in Holden and Ameera's world. When Holden plays billiards at his club with blood on his boots it is because he has sacrificed a goat for his Indian son, giving life for life. When a District Officer remarks that nature is about to 'audit her accounts with a big red pencil' and a passing MP admires the blood-red *dhak*-tree which presages cholera, they underscore the oriental intertwining of death and beauty which is a poignant reality for Holden:

> There are not many unhappinesses so complete as those that are snatched under the shadow of the sword. They sat together and laughed, calling each other openly by every pet name that could

move the wrath of the gods. The city below them was locked up in its own torments. Sulphur fires blazed in the streets; the conches in the Hindu temples screamed and bellowed, for the gods were inattentive in those days.

J. A. V. Chapple remarks that 'Society is by no means slighted, but as with Hardy's work, this story reaches to something at once larger and smaller than Society: human beings seem to suffer from life itself.'[23] Certainly Kipling achieves a strong measure of pathos, and there is something powerfully reminiscent of Hardy in the storm which comes too late to save Ameera, but acts as a metaphor for Holden's grief. The intense emotional pitch is counterpointed by the vivid but impassive Indian scenery, although at least once Kipling strives a little too hard, as when Ameera 'made no sign when Holden entered, because the human soul is a very lonely thing and when it is getting ready to go away, hides itself in a misty borderland where the living may not follow.' This is what one might call a Tolstoyan idea, and it really needs a Tolstoy to execute it. Kipling's briskness makes it sound unconvincing. The tragedy of 'Without Benefit of Clergy' can only demand a relatively detached feeling of pity, not one of cosmic awe. More successful is the brief end of the child, Tota: 'Ameera, wild with terror, watched him through the night, and in the dawning of the second day the life was shaken out of him by fever – the seasonal autumn fever.' The suffering in this story needs to be underplayed because, compared with Hardy, Kipling is a romantic who does not link the sense of pity to a critique of society in any but the most oblique way. The charmed circle within which Holden and Ameera exist is simply annihilated. They are helpless not ultimately, as with the exhausting struggles that Tess or Jude endure, but immediately: they can only sit and watch their fate close in. One can understand why Elliott L. Gilbert finds existentialist ideas at work,[24] but Ameera's romantic assertion that Holden is the only god she has any faith in is hardly good evidence. The story has none of existentialism's capacity for revealing the world as more bizarre and outrageous than we had supposed. The final mood of 'Without Benefit of Clergy' is elegaic, and we are invited to grieve for its characters as individuals struck by misfortune. But if the whole point is that Holden and Ameera withdraw from society, it is still possible to see in the story a reaction to his society on Kipling's part. Kipling uses the illicit relationship of Holden and Ameera to generate a fantasy kingdom of domestic bliss, and one cannot read the story without calling to mind the propensity of numbers of Victorian gentlemen for maintaining two households, the mistress and the wife. As in 'Beyond the Pale' the love affair between white man and black woman vanishes without leaving a trace behind it, but the bleak note on which 'Without Benefit of Clergy' ends seems to register a mute protest at this need for concealment. Once again, Kipling's attitude fluctuates; here between a tragic vision of life and an almost personal hurt. This is not necessarily to criticise: the latter quality has its impact, and it is one that Kipling surely shares with some near-contemporaries like Gissing. Thus, although Kipling approaches his subject here with considerable sensitivity, complete detachment – a Kipling paring his fingernails – is not its primary aesthetic quality. Where it differs from many of the stories concerning men like Holden is also where it shares a quality common to many of the stories in which Kipling sets out to 'illustrate the native feature'. All these stories tend to have about them a 'timeless' air. The native characters in the early volume entitled *In Black and White* and in some stories in *Life's Handicap* frequently enact scenes from legend, with the effect of giving some of them a touch of grandeur to go with their universal simplicity. This is an advance on the Anglo-Indian tradition of humorous ridicule but, unlike Ameera, these protagonists remain ineradicably alien. An early article in the *Civil and Military Gazette* outlines Kipling's basic attitude quite unequivocally.

> He threw back his head and laughed aloud – not with the laughter of civilisation, but the laughter that betrayed his origin – mirth, savage and boisterous, that had nothing in common with gold watch-guard, English clothes, patent trunks or first-class tickets. I confess I liked him better for it. He was of his own people again. Thereafter he spoke and laughed hugely over queer tales of crooked intrigue, in which midnight assignations on housetops, stealthy prowls through narrow blind gullies, feud, lust, and blood were picturesquely mingled.[25]

This westernised – or 'Englishised', as Kipling prefers it – Afghan never appears in Kipling's fiction; and this is hardly surprising, for the journalist here only accepts his existence with the greatest reluctance, and as an aberration from the 'reality'. The reality for

Kipling is the Afghan who describes how he deals with his adulterous wife in 'Dray Wara Yow Dee':

> Then said I: 'Have no fear.' And she bowed her head, and I smote it off at the neck-bone so that it leaped between my feet. Thereafter the rage of my people came upon me, and I hacked off the breasts, that the men of little Malikand might know the crime, and cast the body into the watercourse that flows to Kabul river.

It helps immeasurably, if one is to entertain this piece of bumptious sadism, to have the preconceptions about Afghans of Kipling and his readers. It illustrates at a low level Kipling's adeptness at a kind of pastiche that gives his descriptions a surface resonance – in this case the combination of oriental cruelty with biblical phraseology – but it was universally well received by his contemporaries. The *Athenaeum* reviewer of *In Black and White* unintentionally captures the predictable quality. The stories, he says, 'set before us in contrast the native and his master – the crafty subservience of the one, the contemptuous self-reliance of the other', and he adds that 'another secret of Mr Kipling's success is the directness with which, in an age of over-refined analysis of human motives he deals with the old-world, indestructible themes of love and hate'.[26] Most of the early reviews demonstrate the popularity of this marketing of the archaic and primitive. Lionel Johnson prefers Kipling's natives and common soldiers to the 'strained intensity' of the officers and civilians, and his favourite stories in *Life's Handicap*, after the Mulvaney ones and 'Without Benefit of Clergy', are the 'primaeval' sketches of native life.[27]

'It is the strength of this new story-teller', remarked Kipling's friend Edmund Gosse, 'that he re-awakens in us the primitive emotions of curiosity, mystery, and romance in action. He is the master of a new kind of terrible and enchanting peepshow, and we crowd around him begging for "just one more look".'[28] This strength, of course, is precisely Kipling's flaw. His descriptions of 'native life' are too much of a peepshow – hermetically sealed, set to move in a pre-ordained pattern. Some of the early stories make very plain a tendency that is always there – in the charmed circle of 'Without Benefit of Clergy' and the endless Laws of the Jungle. Compared with the soldier stories, those in which Kipling deals in one way or another with traditional India are used to imply the sahib's perfections rather than his problems. Characteristic is the depiction of the famine-relief hero in 'William the Conqueror':

> He had no desire to make any dramatic entry, but an accident of the sunset ordered it that, when he had taken off his helmet to get the evening breeze, the low light should fall across his forehead, and he could not see what was before him; while one waiting at the tent door beheld, with new eyes, a young man, beautiful as Paris, a god in a halo of golden dust, walking slowly at the head of his flocks, while at his knee ran small naked cupids.

The Indian scene blends into the stuff of popular romance here, and the white man plays his part with a rather bland lustre. But although Kipling consistently portrays an ordered British India that is in harmony with the natural order, much of this work conveys in one way or another a sense of the fragility of all such order, and the extent to which codes and disciplines are straws in the wind. In this context there is a poignancy even to the sense of well-being, eminently suited to the pages of *The Gentlewoman*,[29] that radiates from 'William the Conqueror'. If confidence in the Raj appears to be built into the structures that Kipling adapts from fantasy, legend, and romance, it is capable of being undermined by fear. The 'jungle' that Kipling sometimes perceives is not totally at our command because a part of it is inside us. In the glimpses of this that he provides the Indian teller of tales participates in his own way in the mood of the 'fin-de-siècle'.

5
Kipling and the Eighteen-Nineties

It would be impossible for any study of Kipling to ignore the wide fluctuations in his reputation and the controversy that has surrounded his work as a result of the political commitment that is evident in every phase of his writing. To deal dispassionately with his work is difficult because of this; and the reputation itself has created the temptation to ignore the historical context of the work, and to read it mainly in terms of Kipling's personal life and political convictions.

There is a further obstacle to looking at Kipling in context, because at first glance it does not appear to be a very fruitful approach. It is helpful here to contrast Kipling with his near-contemporary George Gissing. In Kipling's work there appear to be few *positive* correlations with the preoccupations of his contemporaries, whereas the relevance of Gissing's interests to the entire age can be made apparent, as they are in Adrian Poole's *Gissing in Context*.[1] Gissing's sense of malaise as an increasingly faceless social structure combines with a sharpened desire for personal autonomy; his interest in the city as an organism, and in female subjects; his ambivalence towards the class-struggles of the period: all these make it possible for us to trace the links between his work and that of James, Hardy, Moore, Shaw and Wells, as well as to highlight the features that distinguish them from the preceding generation of novelists. Perhaps Gissing is no more a 'representative' figure than Kipling, but his work seems to open immediate avenues for the literary historian.

A Gissing character reminds us of Kipling's own influence on the period. Rolfe, in *The Whirlpool*, is commenting on the *Barrack-Room Ballads*: 'It's the voice of reaction. Millions of men, natural men, revolting against the softness and sweetness of civilisation; men all over the world; hardly knowing what they want and what they don't want . . .'[2] This is part of a widely held view that has come down through literary criticism and comment to the present.

Gissing is at least voicing some of the problems of his age; Kipling is only reacting against them. The history of Kipling criticism is chiefly divided between those who wish to bury him as a minor figure and those who extol his individuality, usually with at least some sympathy for his advocacy of the empire.

Almost from the moment he arrived in London, Kipling was the most consistently popular author of his day, and Gissing complained elsewhere of his 'nefarious appeal to the least creditable instincts of the masses'.[3] Rolfe takes a more balanced, or rather, a more puzzled view. The puzzlement is not with Kipling's 'reactionary' appeal to the masses, but with his own phrase, 'the softness and sweetness of civilisation'; for how could Kipling, the uncrowned laureate of the Empire, author of the jubilee hymn 'Recessional', be *against* civilisation in the radical, disorientating ('hardly knowing what they want and what they don't want') way that this phrase seems to imply? Kipling's role as the chronicler of the Raj, and the values he upheld, might appear straightforward enough, yet many of the contemporary observers who could see beyond his popular success found him a curious, even bewildering figure. 'That little black demon of a Kipling' was Henry James's description in a letter warning Robert Louis Stevenson of Kipling's projected visit to Samoa; to which he added that Kipling was taking literary genius out of the country in his pocket. Stevenson replied in kind, agreeing on Kipling's complete genius, and yet finding Kipling's romantic tales lacking in the very quality one would expect: 'There is no blot of heart's blood and old night'.[4] In the lives of the British in an India that he could bring to life in vivid detail Kipling appeared to have the materials for a fictional epic, and yet, prolific though he was, he seemed to want to give no more than restless glimpses of what he knew. 'True-to-life' as his India was, it had not the solidity that such a grand literary opportunity seemed to warrant. The writers of the metropolis, to whom India was a remote and colourful province, could not be aware of the problems associated with constructing a satisfactory vision of Empire that have emerged from the preceding chapters; nor could they discern the extent to which, as will be argued in this chapter, he was indirectly responding to the cultural and social life of Britain in ways not very dissimilar from theirs.

It is worth looking, to begin with, at the way in which Kipling actually fitted in to the literary community that included many of the reviewers of his own work. After his prolonged voyage from

India via Burma, Hong Kong, Japan, and the United States (where he interviewed Mark Twain) with his friends Professor and Mrs Hill, Kipling arrived at Liverpool on 5 October 1889, and went to London with them. He already had contact with the literary world through two editors with whom he had worked in India. Stephen Wheeler, his first taskmaster in India, was at the *St James Gazette*, and Mowbray Morris, formerly of the *Pioneer*, was editor of *Macmillan's Magazine*, where much of Kipling's work was to appear in the next few years. Andrew Lang immediately took Kipling to the Savile Club. When he was formally admitted to membership a year later his sponsors included Walter Besant, Edmund Gosse, Rider Haggard, Thomas Hardy, Henry James and George Saintsbury. The difficulty was not to make contacts in the literary world, but to resist the pressure to belong to a particular set. Friends, including the especially companionable Rider Haggard, advised him to choose one, but Kipling preferred the contrary advice of Walter Besant.[5] Kipling could be independent to the point of churlishness, but it seems slightly curious that he had so little contact with the 'new conservatives' who wrote for the *New Review*. These were men who realised that the conventions of the mid-Victorian age were changing, and who were interested in new forms of expression and new ideas, but who opposed the selfishness and amorality that they saw in the aesthetic and decadent movement.[6] Under the editorship of Archibald Grove the *New Review*, at the height of the Kipling boom, published none of his work – this at a time when the *Fortnightly Review*, eclectic but often radical, under the editorship of Frank Harris (described by Kipling as 'the one human being that I could on no terms get on with'[7]) was willing to publish Kipling's turgid attack on the state of England under the Liberals entitled 'One View of the Question'. Under the editorship of Kipling's friend W. E. Henley the *New Review* in 1895 belatedly published 'The Song of the Banjo', a piece of verse that amounts to something like self-parody. One senses that perhaps the young journalist from India was insufficiently *upper* middle class to find acceptance in this milieu. The early stories of Simla, the interest in 'low' and barrack-room life, and the excesses of *The Light That Failed* may have aroused a suspicion even among the less traditional that Kipling was somehow not quite a 'gentleman'.

The description 'new conservative' fits William Ernest Henley, the patriotic poet and remarkable editor who published Kipling's ballads in his *Scots Observer*. But Henley too was an 'outsider', who had launched his literary venture from Edinburgh, while his literary tastes ranged far beyond any 'set'. His protegés and acquaintances included Wilde and Shaw, Barrie and Yeats, and at a later date Wells and Conrad. Kipling felt a genuine warmth for Henley, yet even here he was not fully at ease. Henley, he said, was 'not going to come the bullying cripple over me, after I have been in harness all these years' (Henley had a wooden leg).[8] It is unlikely that he mixed easily with the others in Henley's fold, for his antipathies were, to judge by his language, violent, and he paid few courtesies to 'literary lions'. His attitude towards aesthetes and decadents is summed up by this vicious caricature:

> A lean, unshorn, toadstool-coloured young gentleman in a blue cloak which would have been useless on horseback or in a high wind, a dead-leaf silk throat-wrap, and a sort of football jersey that was doing duty as a shirt, threw himself down on the divan and curled his legs in esoteric attitudes.[9]

In the main, Kipling was able to get on with a few generous associates – Besant, Gosse, Haggard, and James – who had no very specific associations themselves. Meanwhile the popular press inevitably made of him an up-and-coming young Bohemian as well as an up-and-coming young writer. An interviewer from *The World* visited Kipling at his rooms in Embankment Chambers in April 1890 and produced an account which makes much of his Indian furnishings and the fez which he affected.

The important point about the situation in which Kipling placed himself in London, until his marriage and departure in 1892, is that he was writing for a living, and had to find or create a market for his work. For a particular literary set there were the *Savoy Magazine* and the famous *Yellow Book*, as well as Henley's *Scots Observer*, all of them stylish productions of limited circulation. But Kipling's work appeared in *Macmillan's Magazine, The Contemporary Review, The Fortnightly Review, Longman's Magazine, Harper's Weekly, Lippincott's Monthly, The English Illustrated, The Idler* and *The Pall Mall Gazette*, to name only a few. He was quite capable at this time of writing to order, penning 'The Ballad of the *Bolivar*' for fifteen guineas in the office of the *St James's Gazette*, and allowing some censorship of 'The Incarnation of Krishna Mulvaney'.[11] When *St Nicholas* magazine was ready for an innocuous fairy story entitled 'The Potted Princess' Kipling could supply one, and likewise when

The Idler (edited by Jerome K. Jerome) could take a contribution, he wrote a harmless farce whose *coup de théâtre* is the inadvertent exposure of a nun's legs on a New York fire escape.[12] 'The White Seal', published in *The Jungle Book* with its final paragraph deleted, began life as an Aesopian look at the Bering Sea dispute between Russia and America for *The Nation*.

The bulk of Kipling's work, however, had to make its way by showing a quality and originality that would distinguish him from the mass of contributors in the 'magazine age' in which he was living. His vogue as an Indian story-teller helped to launch him, but more than this was required to win the critical acclaim that would turn him into a successful author. Writing for the magazines did not by itself confer any status, and the vast increase both of mass-circulation newspapers and of more 'middlebrow' journals was viewed with frequent distaste. Gissing devoted his best-known novel to the evils of *New Grub Street* (1891), while Mrs Oliphant saw nothing but vanity in the new trend: 'It is a common thing to hear said in our day that people read nothing but magazines ... we have sometimes thought that the real cause of the constant multiplication might be that nobody in the present day feels called upon to read, while everyone attempts to write, and desires to see him or herself in print.' There was nothing controversial about Wilde's comment that 'In old days books were written by men of letters and read by the public. Nowadays books are written by the public and read by nobody.'[13] All of Kipling's great contemporaries also published their work in magazine form, but he is perhaps remarkable for the extent to which he belonged to the magazine world while simultaneously emerging as a major literary figure, approved by an editorial in *The Times* (25 March 1890).

Edmund Gosse was quick to produce an explanation for the importance of Kipling's work: 'Between excess of psychological analysis and excess of superhuman romance, there was a great void in the world of Anglo-Saxon fiction. It is this void which Mr Kipling has filled by his exotic realism and his rendering of unhackneyed experience.'[14] The general sense that literature had lost its 'centre' and gone over to extremes was widespread. J. A. Spender, in his attack on *The New Fiction* (1895) sets up a different but related dichotomy:

> The most respectable of the Old Critics seem to have frankly

given up the task of criticising the modern social novel. . . . In fiction they call for romance, adventure, blood; and to some of us it seems they will take any quantity of the last commodity in composition for the first two. But while the Old Critics cry "blood" the New ones reply "flesh and blood", and to some of us again it seems that when they say "flesh and blood" they mean flesh.[15]

The critical thinking of the day was mixed up with moral considerations, even when the critic was not an overt moralist. The many reviewers who praised Kipling's 'manly' or 'masculine' style were also implying that he had a steady, rounded view of life. The currency of the term in this sense is confirmed by Mrs Oliphant who, after disposing of such deviants as George Moore and Thomas Hardy, commends her contemporaries thus:

> We may add with pride and gratitude that these entirely manly writers, troubled by no feminine qualms as to propriety, have very rarely found it necessary to resort to those unwholesome qualities of vice and so-called passion in which the novelists of France have lost themselves as in an enchanted labyrinth. The larger atmosphere of human life, with all its tragedies and problems, has sufficed and nobly occupied them – the great and broad and ever-varied world which was enough for Shakespeare and happily remains so always for English art.[16]

After a few initial suspicions that he was either too risqué, or else, like Haggard, making it all up, the critics had sold themselves on the idea that Kipling was 'manly' in a notion that implied both their liking for his patriotism and gospel of work, and the implication that he fulfilled the requirement of creating an 'organic', broad and varied fictional world. For this reason references to Shakespeare and Dickens, the Victorians' twin gods, are common in the early reviews. *The Light That Failed* produced some check to this response, and with *Life's Handicap* there is a simultaneous recognition that Kipling has passed from phenomenon to solid man of letters, and puzzlement that his achievement does not feel more solid.

We can now turn to the ways in which India as a subject helped Kipling to fill such a niche in the literary sensibility of the nineties, as well as to comment on the British social life that he was now experiencing fully for the first time. A popular novel of the eighties gives some idea of what could and had been done with India at the time. The American novelist F. Marion Crawford's *Mr Isaacs: A Tale of Modern India* appeared in 1882, and was reissued in a cheaper edition by Macmillan in 1889. Like so much colonial fiction of the popular variety it is a novel with a thesis, which addresses itself to the issue of the status of women in society. Mr Isaacs is a wealthy and thoroughly anglicised merchant of Iranian extraction, but still a practising Muslim, whom the narrator (a journalist, coincidentally) seeks to persuade on the question of women's role in Victorian life. The ideal is

> A woman who, as she learned your strange story, should weep for the pains you suffered and rejoice for the difficulties overcome, who should understand your half-spoken thoughts and proudly sympathise in your unuttered aspirations; in whom you might see the twin nature to your own, and detect the strong spirit and the brave soul, half revealed through the feminine gentleness and modesty that clothe her as a garment. . . . Suppose you married her – not to lock her up in an indolent atmosphere of rosewater, narghyles, and sweetmeats, to die of inanition or to pester you to death with complaints and jealousies and inopportune caresses; but to be with you and help your life when you most need help. . . . Would you not believe she had a soul?[17]

To begin with Isaacs (who has three wives) is understandably sceptical about this picture of bliss. Almost immediately, however, he falls in love with a young Englishwoman, who effects the desired transformation in his point of view. Unfortunately the young lady catches fever and dies while Isaacs is unavoidably absent from her side (he is obliged to rescue the deposed Amir of Afghanistan), and the novel ends with the intervention of his mysterious Buddhist mentor, who elaborately assures us that the marriage will take place in heaven.

Crawford's approach to British India in this soft-centred romance has nothing in common with Kipling's. The India he describes is evidently the product of a rather superficial and genteel liberalism. The luxury and idleness of white life in India with its plethora of native servants is pointed out, but if the Indians are represented as generally resourceful and hard working the English are all brave and courteous, although the traditional sahib is mildly lampooned in the figure of 'Mr Currie Ghyrkins, the Collector of Mudnugger'. While Crawford appears to know just what it is like to ride in a tonga or how natives cook on a journey, his description beside Kipling's is very laboured and plain. Crawford and Kipling do, however, use some of the same types, and play with the same distinction between Aryan and non-Aryan peoples – Isaacs being only a shade less 'white' than a European. It is noticeable, all the same, that the absurd plot conveniently aborts the proposed inter-racial marriage. Different as they are, both authors use India to depart a little from social and fictional norms without actually breaking any taboos. Allowing for their extreme variance from each other in terms of originality, *Mr Isaacs* and 'Without Benefit of Clergy' both use the Indian setting to comment on the Victorian institute of marriage. India can be a potential sounding board in a way that it is not in another famous, but much earlier novel. Philip Meadows Taylor's *Confessions of a Thug* (1837) is the fictionalised autobiography of the leader of one of the bands of religious stranglers dedicated to Kali, the goddess of destruction, who still roamed India in the early part of the nineteenth century. The novel is remarkable for its treatment of thuggee on a purely phenomenal level. The white sahib is a passive auditor with a pragmatic desire to stamp out thuggee in the interests of trade, and less than total confidence in his ability to do so. Thuggee is evil, of course, but there is no overt apostrophising of western virtue and oriental vice, and the contrast affords a valuable insight into the way in which the self-consciousness that came with the founding of the Raj and the new vocabulary of imperial duty and responsibility informs the portrayal of India by Kipling.

Although very little literature came out of Anglo-India itself there was, even by the middle of the century, a tradition according to which India acted as a moral touchstone. For most of Kipling's readers to think of India was probably to think of two characters in the novels of Thackeray – Colonel Newcome in *The Newcomes* (1855), and Jos Sedley in *Vanity Fair* (1848). Colonel Newcome is a slightly naive but altogether virtuous character; generous and warm-hearted. Jos Sedley is equally naive, but he is a 'nabob' in whom India has brought out a surfeit of vanity, sloth and cowardice. Both characters function as touchstones for the other characters in their respective novels. Jos Sedley is as hopelessly out of place following Wellington's army to Waterloo as he possibly could be, and the honest colonel is equally lost among the social pretensions of his London relatives. The panoply of characters in *The Newcomes* are self-interested or goodnatured in different degrees, but none can attain the complete freedom from socially-acquired mannerism and vice that distinguishes the colonel. Conversely, in *Vanity Fair*, the need for respect and a place in society prevents any other character sinking into the state of infantile degeneracy epitomised by Jos. Flora Annie Steel's *On the Face of the Waters*, published in 1898, continues to reflect this tendency to portray Anglo-Indian characters in terms of their clearly defined moral qualities. Her story focuses on a resourceful loner who, like a number of Kipling heroes, dons native disguise while remaining impeccably 'British' in outlook, and contrasts him with the boorish rake to whom the heroine has the misfortune to be married. India is again used to highlight civilised and Christian virtues in the key confrontation between the heroine, Kate, and the hero's loyal servant, Tara:

> "The *mem* is afraid", cried Tara exultantly. "So be it! I will go back and tell the master. Tell him I was right and he is wrong for all the English he chattered. I will tell him the *mem* is not *suttee* – how could she be – ".
> The old taunt roused many memories, and made Kate ready to risk anything. "I am coming, Tara – but where?" She stood facing the tall figure in crimson, a tall figure also, in white, her hands full of the white roses she had gathered.[18]

The contrast between white and crimson, Christian purity and heathen custom, is used to present the British victory over the mutineers as one of moral rectitude. Kate, of course, gets her man, as her husband tactfully kills himself, and Tara commits a symbolic act of suttee on the burning ruins of Delhi.

The British view of India examined in Chapter 1 finds India to be darkly exotic, corrupt and potentially corrupting but it also tends to see it in terms of a clear and simple antithesis. The situation of the British is forever reducible to the struggle of Christianity with heathenism. It is surely fair to say that Kipling is influenced by a tradition which tends to affirm that India sets examples, but he is able to set examples while writing in a different idiom – one which at times owes something to 'aesthetic' writing – and from a viewpoint that has moved away from the moral self-confidence of Victorian traditionalism. It is worth returning briefly here to

'Love-o'-Women' as perhaps the most striking example of such a combination. Within the enormous range of his reading, Kipling had a special affection for Elizabethan and Jacobean literature, and it is no surprise to find that the epigraph to 'Love-o'-Women' comes from John Ford's tragicomedy *The Lover's Melancholy*. It is 'a lamentable tale of things/Done long ago, and ill done.'[19] Certainly Ford is an appropriate author to quote from here, for his drama focuses very much on the destructive power of sexual appetites and the consequences of their denial or indulgence. There is something actually reminiscent of Ford in the terse, graphic phraseology of 'Love-o'-Women': ' "Fwhat do you do here?" she sez, an her voice wint up. 'Twas like bells tollin' before. "Time was whin you were quick enough wid your words, – you that talked me down to hell. Are ye dumb now?" ' Mulvaney concludes that 'Mackie that's dead an' in hell is the lucky man' with a grimness to match Ford's couplet – 'Here's fatal sad presages: but 'tis just/He dies by murder that hath lived in lust.'[20] In Ford as in Kipling vice is culpable but it is also, in a way entirely foreign to simple Victorian notions of how to maintain one's virtue, deeply and fearfully contagious.

Kipling may possibly have discovered Ford for himself in his schooldays, but his work was publicly rediscovered in the 1880s when Henry Vizetelly was persuaded to bring out a new popular edition of the 'Old Dramatists' by Havelock Ellis, who edited the series and wrote in his introduction to Ford's *Best Plays* that

> This man writes of women not as a dramatist nor as a lover, but as one who had searched intimately and felt with instinctive sympathy the fibres of their hearts. He was an analyst; he strained the limits of his art to the utmost; he foreboded new ways of expression. Thus he is less nearly related to the men who wrote *Othello* and *A Woman Killed with Kindness*, and Valentinian, than to those poets and artists of the naked human soul, the writer of *Le Rouge et Le Noir*, and the yet greater writer of *Madame Bovary*.[21]

Ford had thus been claimed as a 'contemporary'; a writer on the side of modern trends in literature, for whom the study of women was essential as it was for the novelists of the late nineteenth century. When Henry James became disillusioned with Kipling it ocurred to him that his tales said 'almost nothing of the complicated soul or of the female form'.[22] Despite its importance to the serious novelists, 'psychological analysis' in fiction was regarded with some suspicion, on the grounds that it implied a refusal properly to condemn the Emma Bovaries of the world and, rather worse, to consider them suitable subjects for fiction in the first place. As we have seen, an observer like Edmund Gosse – hardly adverse to probing the psyche – could consider the tendency excessive. The novel form, and by implication the detailed study of character, was still regarded by many as the true test of the young Kipling's abilities, and in *The Light That Failed* he certainly attempted a degree of psychological analysis. Unfortunately he did so with a chronic lack of objectivity.

A central problem with *The Light That Failed* is that the characters never emerge to become more than a combination of ill-assorted types which Kipling either admires or detests. In Dick Heldar, the hero, we have a reckless man of action who spends the greater portion of the novel absorbed in self-pity. Despite his faults, the pathos with which Kipling invests him precludes his being considered a modern 'anti-hero'. Dick is a demonic artist who sketches in brothels in Port Said, but he is also an entirely ordinary young man who wants to get married: 'Dick considered rapidly the murkiness of an average man's life. There was nothing in the review to fill him with a sense of virtue.' (7) It is the latter side of Dick that produces the most successful passages:

> He had risen to his feet, and stood in the shadow of the gun, looking down at the girl. The very short winter afternoon had worn away, and before they knew, the winter moon was walking the untroubled sea. Long ruled lines of silver showed where a ripple of the rising tide was turning over the mud-banks. The wind had dropped, and in the intense stillness they could hear a donkey cropping the frosty grass many yards away. A faint beating like that of a muffled drum, came out of the moon-haze.
> 'What's that?' said Maisie quickly. 'It sounds like a heart beating. Where is it?' (7)

The quiet irony with which Dick's hopes are shattered here, and the wonderfully crisp and clear descriptive language, are out of key with the novel as a whole. The final catastrophe in which Dick's masterpiece is destroyed is stage-managed with an acid-hued irony that is derivative of Hardy, but Dick has acquired none of the sympathetic traits of a Hardy hero or heroine, and as he travels to his death in the Sudan, his delight in violence for its own sake is alarmingly endorsed.

> 'Hrrmph!' said the machine gun through all its five noses as the subaltern drew the lever home. The empty cartridges clashed on the floor and the smoke blew back through the truck. There was indiscriminate firing at the rear of the train, a return fire from the darkness without and unlimited howling. Dick stretched himself on the floor, wild with delight at the sounds and the smells.
> 'God is very good – I never thought I'd hear this again. Give 'em hell, men. Oh, give 'em hell!' he cried. (15)

This is a sadistic passage certainly, and by no means the first in the book, but it is, up to a point, conscious of its own sadism. Dick's pleasure is portrayed as almost bestial, and the scene is a deliberate outlet for the frustrations that he has experienced in London. Kipling could have stuck, as his mother apparently wished, to the version of the novel that appeared in *Lippincott's*, in which Maisie finally discovers, when she sees Dick in his blindness, that she loves him.[23] This ending makes a nonsense of the novel's one strength: the idea that Maisie's 'unnatural' cruelty in refusing Dick is part of nature's pattern of ceaseless conflict. Maisie is, in Ruskinian fashion, Dick's 'Queen', but he nevertheless regards his wooing in the light of an internecine struggle: 'Oh, my little darling, if ever I break you, somebody will have a very bad time of it . . . ' (6). Maisie herself has the making of a credible, though preferably a minor, character, in that her lack of warmth chimes well enough with the rather tame and talentless creature she is fated to be. But just as it sometimes seems that Dick is heroic simply because he is a war-artist, so Maisie's weakness seems somehow to be bound up with her addiction to the fashionable artistic salons. 'Toadstool' is again a key word as Dick quite skilfully teases Maisie about art:

> Once when I was out in the Soudan I went over some ground that we had been fighting on for three days. There were twelve hundred dead; and we hadn't time to bury them. ... It looked just like a bed of horrible toadstools in all colours, and – I'd never seen men in bulk go back to their beginnings before. So I began to understand that men and women were only material to work with, and that what they said or did was of no consequence.(7)

Maisie is predictably horrified by this purely 'artistic' and 'amoral' way of looking at things. Against the decadents' exploration of the artificial and unnatural, Dick makes the point that the world outside London offers enough strange sights to the artist who is prepared to go and look for them. Elsewhere, Kipling produced an able parody of Ernest Dowson's 'Blue Roses'. But there is an odd anomaly between Dick's painting of a battle-scene, which we overhear two veteran soldiers praising for its accuracy, and the work that Dick is actually described in the act of painting – his 'Melancolia', the Port Said brothel, and the painting done at sea which features a 'sort of Negroid-Jewess-Cuban; with morals to match.' If Kipling had no sympathy with the aim of experiencing life in the manner of art, he did hanker after certain types of experience in a way characteristic of the period. This, however, makes it no easier to accept his characterisation of this period as balanced or plausible. The novel sums up Kipling's refusal to accept or approve the way of life he found in London, but he has no time to spare for examining either the daily round of the lower classes or the upper-class world of corrupt artists and publishers from which the villains of his piece are supposed to step. The hero's childhood traumas, closely based on Kipling's experience of boarding out in Southsea, are the context provided for his later extremes of behaviour, but there is no context in which to place the civilisation at which he rages, and no possibility of evaluating Kipling's obvious sympathy with him. The attempt to probe the psychological and artistic state of London from an Anglo-Indian viewpoint cannot survive Kipling's almost pathological dislike of his subject.

Little as he had to say about theories of art, as opposed to theories of artistic inspiration, Kipling clearly counterposed some not very clear notion of 'realism' to the kind of contemporary art that he disliked. Dick's battle-scenes are contrasted with what one of the characters in *The Light That Failed* describes as the 'chromo-litholeo-margarine fake' – the battle-scene in which the soldiers have polished boots and clean uniforms. He is capable of perceiving the difference between this kind of distortion and the 'distortions' of impressionism, but he is not much interested in doing so, since *both* strike him as distorted in unacceptable ways. After a few months in London he had got to know the music halls, and he lauded their wholesome vulgarity by comparing it with the vulgarity he detected in the West End theatres:

At one place the lodging-house servant was an angel, and her mother a Madonna; at a second they sounded the loud timbrel o'er a whirl of bloody axes, mobs, and brown paper castles, and said it was not a pantomime, but Art; at a third everybody grew fabulously rich and fabulously poor every twenty minutes, which was confusing; at a fourth they discussed the Nudities and Lewdities in false-palate voices supposed to belong to the aristocracy and that tasted copper in the mouth; at a fifth they merely climbed up the walls and threw furniture at each other, which is notoriously the custom of spinsters and small parsons.[24]

The fourth and fifth on his list are recognisably plays of a type akin to the work of Wilde and Ibsen respectively, and although Kipling does not go much beyond mere abuse, the abuse is directed at the lack of 'realism' of these unfortunate productions, rather than at their 'immorality'. A rather crude realism, which insists that there is no difficulty in taking things as they are, is apt, unless the artist is exceptional, to remain bound to the status quo. The exceptional 'realist' or 'naturalist' figure of Kipling's time was Emile Zola, to whom two young Anglo-Indians improbably, perhaps, refer in Kipling's early story 'At Twenty-Two'. Georg Lukacs argues that the kind of new realism Zola represented was a consequence of the distancing of writers from political and social life as a result of their new role as commentators for the newly evolved bourgeoisie to which they belonged. Thus 'Zola's naturalistic "experimental" novels were ... merely attempts to find a method by which the writer, now reduced to a mere spectator, could again realistically master reality.'[25] In effect, as Lukacs goes on to point out, Zola's attitude to reality was similar to a newspaper reporter.

If the advantage of the approach was that it could bring to light areas of public life that were usually ignored, the danger was that the writer might compensate for his attitude of spectatorship by making a 'spectacle' of his subject, as Kipling does in his portrayal of the East End in 'The Record of Badalia Herodsfoot'. The story was one of the progenitors of the nineties' vogue for 'slum-fiction', along with Arthur Morrison's 'A Street', which appeared a year later.[26] The greyly neutral tone of Morrison's observations, and especially the careful recording of different degrees of squalor and respectability in 'A Street' provide an important contrast with Kipling's apocalyptic style in 'Badalia Herodsfoot'. Interest in the East End in particular had been growing since the 1870s, and in 1884

Toynbee Hall was founded in order to bring middle-class culture and philanthropy to the deprived classes, an approach satirised by Kipling in his portrayal of 'Mrs Jessel of the Tea-Cup Board'. The working class had begun to figure prominently in the novels of Gissing and Walter Besant, brother-in-law of the social reformer Annie. The culmination of this new awareness can be seen in the publication in 1889 of *East London*, the first volume of Charles Booth's monumental survey, *The Life and Labour of the People in London*. Because the forms he used were the short story and the ballad adapted from the music halls, Kipling could focus exclusively on working-class life in a way that Besant and Gissing could not, and there is also a new refusal to dilute this life, a breaking up of the stereotypes of an earlier age – Dickens' Sam Weller and the mid-Victorian ' 'Arry', the uncouth but stout-hearted and fervently patriotic figure from *Punch*. In the *Barrack-Room Ballads* Kipling's soldiers record their attitudes with the same unbowdlerised vigour that came across on the music-hall stage. In the stories the use of dialect sometimes achieves a specifically working-class eloquence – 'Though i' them days, By for God, I never seed bad ale', says Learoyd – though the way in which Mulvaney's colourful language plays up to us is a little suspect.

Certainly Kipling does not impose middle-class attitudes and values on these characters, but he scarcely takes them on their own terms either, for the implication is that these people are *incapable* of acquiring such values. Their way of life is regarded as alien to the larger society, and they are a group permanently cast out from genuine civilisation. It is striking that the working-class, in Kipling's work, always appear as a caged *minority*. In the absence of the saving institution of the British army, it is in 'The Record of Badalia Herodsfoot' that the working-class world is pictured as one of anarchic degradation. Gunnison Street is a sulphurous hell, its monotony a matter not of the inward quality of life, but of the writhing in the outward postures of fighting, drunkenness, and disease that festoon the scene. It is the kind of violent squalor where 'The scrofulous babes multiplied like the green scum on the untopped water cisterns'. In this setting we can as easily infer that a murder will be committed as we can in the Dickens of *Martin Chuzzlewit* or *Oliver Twist*:

> Then Tom took more drink till his drunkenness rolled back and stood off from him as a wave rolls back and stands off the wreck it

will swamp. .... Looking down his past, he beheld that he was justified of all his actions so entirely and perfectly that if Badalia had in his absence dared to lead a blameless life he would smash her for not having gone wrong.

The murder itself is almost sickening in its violent detail.

The preconceptions about Indians that Kipling is used to exploiting are easily transferable to his East End. While odious soul-saving is caricatured, the practically-minded relief workers Brother Victor and Eustace Hanna find a comradeship in adverse conditions that mirrors Kipling's portraits of Anglo-Indian civilians. The best of the relief-workers is Badalia herself because she knows Gunnison Street from the inside, but also because she has within her the 'sacred fever of the administrator'. Badalia is really *too* perfect. Even her room is a haven of orderliness and clean sheets, and her administrative fever immediately makes her look down on those around her. It is not, of course, that the contrast between Badalia and her oafish husband seems unconvincing or untrue to what we know of the East End of the period, but the particular way in which Badalia is made to stand out indicates a degree of manipulation on Kipling's part. Her fluffy fringe and the dark, flaming eyes beneath it, recur through the story as indications of her sexual vigour. As she dies, and relinquishes Eustace Hanna to Sister Eva, the eyes are covered up to indicate this resignation, which adds further poignancy to the death-scene:

> If Tom 'ad come back, which 'e never did, I'd ha' been like the rest — sixpence for the beef-tea for the baby, an' a shilling for layin' out the baby. You've seen it in the books, Mister 'Anna. That's what it is; an o' course you couldn't never 'ave nothing to do with me. But a woman she wishes as she looks . . .

Heroine though she is, Badalia behaves in sexual matters like her rival Jenny, and is enmeshed in the customs of Gunnison Street which, the narrator remarks, 'do not differ from those of the Barralong.' The vigorous Badalia, clearly contrasted with the quiet but love-inspiring sister Eva, in fact epitomises a new type of heroine that had begun to appear in fiction. Havelock Ellis, writing in 1883, identified the Victorian convention by which 'women are considered as moral forces, centrifugal tendencies providentially adapted to balance the centripetal tendencies of men', and had remarked that Hardy's women were almost the opposite to this, being 'made up of more or less untamed instincts for both love and admiration'.[27] This new moral type can surely be identified especially with one physical type, for Hardy's Eustacia Vye springs immediately to mind: 'She had the passions and instincts which make a model goddess, that is, those which make not quite a model woman . . . . She had Pagan eyes, full of nocturnal mysteries, and their light as it came and went and came again, was partially hampered by their oppressive lids and lashes.'[28] Badalia is very evidently of Eustacia's type, but it seems rather convenient for Kipling that she is so clearly confined to her own primitive social milieu.

In view of the apparent care that Kipling took to produce acceptable female types, and to place those that might be unacceptable on the margins of society, it is slightly surprising that a significant number of reviewers regarded Kipling's treatment of women with positive distaste. The focus of their attention was *The Light That Failed*, but they did not regard it as an isolated case. Dick Heldar behaves like a 'cad' with women, according to the *Saturday Review*, and on the same tack Ernest Newman in the *University Magazine* concluded that Kipling's 'mental processes are abnormal rather than anything else'.[29] Yet, as Max Beerbohm pointed out, Dick takes the conventional attitude of worship to hilarious lengths when he anxiously reflects that 'Maisie's a bilious little body'.[30] This response was by no means universal: Mrs Oliphant was enchanted by Dick Heldar, while Lionel Johnson found *The Light That Failed* 'finely and desperately logical'. For Julian Hawthorne Kipling was 'manly and masculine and consequently has an intense appreciation of the feminine in nature: he never touches a woman but we feel the thrill of sex. Mr Thomas Hardy has the same faculty in this regard.'[31] Kipling was, of course, rapped over the knuckles for his ostensibly 'smoking-room' output – 'one longs for the more genial cynicism of a Thackeray', commented the *Athenaeum* – but the frequent element of distaste goes deeper than this. Both favourable and unfavourable responses reflect the reviewers' unending concern with female characters, even in an author who clearly did not specialise in them. It may be that the underlying note of desperation that has become apparent in Kipling's writing is revealed to his contemporaries by his fictional treatment of women, insofar as it raises a doubt about the confident, 'manly' persona he projects.

Kipling's world is, of course, a predominantly masculine one, in which the 'feminine in nature' exists chiefly on a metaphorical level – in the dark, passive, and fundamentally irrational Orient, as later in Kipling's fascination with seafaring. The extent to which Kipling, uniquely in literature, describes men going about their work, has been eloquently described by C. S. Lewis. This is marred by Kipling's 'unwearied knowingness' and his obsession with the 'Inner Ring' of professional cliques, but nevertheless 'The rhythms of work – boots slogging along a road, the Harrild and the Hoe devouring "their league-long paper-bale", the grunting of a water wheel – echo through Kipling's verse and prose as through no other man's.'[32] However, socialist critics in particular have been rather prone to assume that Kipling's use of the rhythms of work entails an attentiveness to ordinary working people.[33] In fact what Kipling chiefly describes, soldiers apart, are the attitudes of the professional classes on the one hand, and the movements of machinery unmediated by human labour on the other. His conclusion about the condition of the working-class in London is that 'the rough timber of a very great army drifts unhewn through the slime of their streets'.[34] His reaction to working class organisations is embodied in the ill-tempered attack entitled 'A Walking Delegate'. Meanwhile people of any description are absent from '.007' and 'The Ship that Found Herself', as they are from the more obvious political fables of a later date, 'The Mother Hive' and 'Below the Mill Dam'. The Indian Civilian's work, of course, is centred on controlling his subordinates. The native population, alternatively intransigent and elusive, is the hardest of materials to work.

A more promising representative figure is McAndrew, Kipling's ship's engineer, whose dedication to his engines is equalled by his contempt for those who never get their hands dirty. But McAndrew is the skilled man, an ambiguous representative of workers in general. Britain, moreover, was in the grip of a romantic attachment to technology that included the upper classes. Engineering was the choice of seventy-five per cent of boys at one public school in the 1880s.[35] Certainly McAndrew's Calvinist litany would have gone down well enough in the public schools:

While, out o' touch o' vanity, the sweatin' thrust-block says:
"Not unto us the praise, or man – not unto us the praise!"
Now a' together, hear them lift their lesson – theirs and mine:
"Law, Order, Duty an' Restraint, Obedience, Discipline!"
                                    (McAndrew's Hymn – 1893)

It is only at the most abstract level that Kipling champions all those who work, but in 'The Sons of Martha' he adopts a somewhat hectoring tone: 'They do not preach that their God will rouse them a little before the nuts work loose./ They do not teach that His pity allows them to leave their job when they damn-well choose.' He is clearly addressing the supervisory grades, not the proletariat. Less crudely expressed, Kipling's emphasis on devotion and discipline has made a strong appeal to people of all persuasions, including a severe critic like H. G. Wells,[36] and 'If' is still part of the furniture of English life. Kipling reminds us often that work is the only panacea for most of life's ills, and we can admire the forbidding truth of the inscription that John Lockwood carved for his son: 'The night cometh, wherein no man can work'. If working life is Kipling's forte, it is in oriental settings that it gains from being interconnected with loneliness and uncertainty.

The rhythms of work are built into a self-supporting system in this monumental description from 'The Bridge-Builders':

> The river was very low, and on the dazzling white sand between the three centre piers stood squat cribs of railway sleepers, filled within and daubed without with mud, to support the last of the girders as those were riveted up. In the little deep water left by the drought, an overhead crane travelled to and fro along its spile-pier, jerking sections of iron into place, snorting and backing and grunting as an elephant grunts in the timber-yard. Riveters by the hundred swarmed about the lattice side-work and the iron roof of the railway line, hung from invisible staging under the bellies of the girders, clustered round the throats of the piers, and rode on the overhang of the footpath-stanchions; their fire-pots and the spurts of flame that answered each hammer-stroke showing no more than pale yellow in the sun's glare. East and west and north and south the construction-trains rattled and shrieked up and down the embankments, the piled trucks of brown and white stone banging behind them till the side-boards were unpinned, and with a roar and a grumble a few more thousand tons of material were thrown out to hold the river in place.

Findlayson, the engineer in charge, has a dream in which a convocation of Hindu gods discuss whether the Ganges should be allowed to destroy the bridge, and conclude that it, as indeed the

Empire, and human activity itself, are mere illusion; the 'dream of Brahm'. J. M. S. Tompkins explicates this as follows:

> The abyss is more than death. It is, what it is to all of us, the whole mystery of the state of man; and since to Kipling man, and especially European man, and more especially the Englishman of the professional classes, is the creature who works, it is in connection with the work of man that the abyss opens its gulf on the rim or in the middle of his tales.[37]

Certainly we sense this abyss in the tale, but it is not conveyed by the dream sequence alone. Although it asserts the mutability of man's works, the dream does not prevent a celebration of those works, just as the lines of 'Recessional'

> Far-called, our navies melt away;
>   On dune and headland sinks the fire:
> Lo, all our pomp of yesterday
>   Is one with Nineveh and Tyre!
> Judge of the Nations, spare us yet,
>   Lest we forget – lest we forget.

express the grandeur of the achievement even as they counsel humility. In 'The Bridge-Builders' the sense of precariousness is implicit in the construction-site itself, despite the characteristically precise and purposive way in which Kipling makes the entire description bear down on its final phrase – 'to hold the river in place.' Saving this sense of purpose, the site has the anonymity and bustle of a great city, and it is this concealed image that starts off the underlying edge of anxiety that gnaws at Findlayson. 'The dominant images associated with the city as a totality in the 1880s are those of intransigence, of immovable and impenetrable relationships and structures ... outside the sphere of the single room, it has become increasingly difficult to see human beings other than in the mass.'[38] This structure of feeling is certainly one that Kipling shared in when he came to London. Dick Heldar, looking out as Kipling must have looked over Charing Cross from his rooms, shrinks in scale for a moment against it, despite his overweening 'God, what a city to loot!' In his own youth the mysteries of night-time Lahore and Calcutta had served Kipling as an image that he enhanced with James Thomson's *The City of*

Dreadful Night. As it came to seem strange and impenetrable to artists and writers, London could also become exotic, as it does in the 'fin-de-siècle' sketches of Hubert Crackanthorpe: 'A sullen glow throbs overhead: golden will o' wisps are threading their shadowy groupings of gaunt-limbed trees; and the dull, distant rumour of feverish London waits on the still night air.'[39] In *Esther Waters* George Moore conveys Esther's mood of fear and bewilderment by creating around her an 'oriental' London of floating minarets and submerged squalor:

> A true London of the water's edge – a London of theatres, music-halls, wine-shops, public-houses – the walls painted various colours, nailed over with huge gold lettering; the pale air woven with delicate wire, a gossamer web underneath which the crowd moved like lazy flies, one half watching the perforated spire of St. Mary's, and all the City spires behind it now growing cold in the east; the other half seeing the spire of St. Martin's above the chimney pots aloft in a sky of cream-pink. Stalwart policemen urged along groups of slattern boys and girls; and after vulgar remonstrance these took the hint and disappeared down strange passages.[40]

Reversing the process, Kipling asserts control over the 'city' by displacing it to India and putting it under Findlayson's control. But cornerstone of the Empire though it is, the Kashi bridge is never visualised in its entirety in the story, and Findlayson's fear for it is strikingly conveyed as a fear of *inward* collapse, as from some fatal disease:

> For himself the crash meant everything – everything that made a hard life worth the living. They would say, the men of his profession – he remembered the half-pitying things that he himself had said when Lockhart's big water-works burst and broke down in brick heaps and sludge, and Lockhart's spirit broke in him and he died.

There is here a rare use of hesitancy and of imagery that does not seek to define its emotion too precisely. The context of sensitivity to the city in the writing of the period makes it possible to detect moods and meanings in Kipling's work that he does not confront directly, and to propose that there are occasions on which he conveys almost the opposite of what he sets out to say. A striking example in his account of his first weeks in London in *Something of Myself* (4):

That period was all, as I have said, a dream, in which it seemed that I could push down walls, walk through ramparts and stride across rivers. Yet I was so ignorant, I never guessed when the great fogs fell that trains could take me to light and sunshine a few miles outside London. Once I faced the reflection of my own face in the jet-black mirror of the window-panes for five days. When the fog thinned, I looked out and saw a man standing opposite the pub where the barmaid lived. Of a sudden his breast turned dull red like a robin's, and he crumpled, having cut his throat.

The book is as scrupulously and tightly controlled as his fiction, but the episode of the suicide surely tells a different story from the triumphal progress of the young author. The reality may have borne more resemblance at times to the sensations recorded by Walter Besant in his autobiography.

> No one appeared to know how desperately miserable an evening in lodgings may be. I have sat with my books before me while the silence grew more and more intolerable, rising up all round as a cloud hiding the rest of the world. When my nerves would stand it no longer, I have taken my hat and rushed out into the streets.[41]

It is, at any rate, a characteristic of Dick Heldar's to vent his frustrations in the streets and parks. The sense of isolation is most successfully handled in 'The Disturber of Traffic', in which the central character, unlike Findlayson, suffers a real defeat. As if to compensate for this, the story of Dowse's breakdown is framed in the recollections of an entirely sane lighthouse keeper on the English coast. The story opens with a fog, the most common of symbols for a state of mental oppression (it is carelessly tossed into Kipling's uncollected 'The Lamentable Comedy of Willow Wood' for this purpose.) Anticipating the story to come, the fog in this case is also conquered – both by lighthouse technology, and by the restrained aestheticism of Kipling's language as 'The pencils of the Light marched staggeringly across tilted floors of white cloud.' The unfortunate Dowse is denied such power and security on his rickety floating light in the Java seas, and after a year the isolation begins to play tricks on his imagination:

Then, he told me, his head began to feel streaky from looking at the tides so long. He said there was long streaks of white running inside it; like wallpaper that hadn't been properly pasted up, he said. The streaks, they would run with the tides, north and south, accordin' to them currents, and he'd lie down on the planking – it was a screw-pile light – with his eyes to a crack and watch the water streaking through the piles just so quiet as hogwash.

Ostensibly the story treats Dowse's descent into madness as a purely occupational hazard. Dowse himself appears in a partly comic light; his collapse as a personal failing, albeit under stress. But there are in the story the glimmerings of a deeper significance and a conception of Dowse's predicament as more universal. What unnerves him is the absence of any human scale to relate to, and it is this that he creates by blocking the fairway with wreck-buoys until, as a ship's captain remarks, ' "The place is like Regent Street of a hot summer night" '. The bobbing lights image the pathos of civilisation, set against the 'flamin', topplin' volcano' in the background. There is tension between sympathy for this aspect of the human condition and impatience with it, and with the Dowse whose mental horizon compares the streaking tide with wallpaper.

'The Disturber of Traffic' was very well received, and many reviewers of *Many Inventions* considered it the best story in the volume. It is written with great elegance and poise, at a time when elegance and poise were in fashion, and at its centre the dull unromantic streakiness in Dowse's head reflects very well the fin-de-siècle malaise. In a famous passage in *Middlemarch* George Eliot had written that

> If we had a keen vision and feeling of all ordinary human life, it would be like hearing the grass grow and the squirrel's heart-beat, and we should die of that roar which lies on the other side of silence. As it is, the quickest of us walk about well wadded with stupidity.[42]

Increasingly, the novelists of the eighties and nineties were coming to question the necessity of such wadding. For Thomas Hardy's Tess and Jude, the stupidities of the social organism have devastating effects on their sensitive natures. In these decades generally, 'For Gissing and Rutherford and Hardy as for Symonds, "wakefulness" becomes a positive activity.'[43] Though the ways in which 'wakefulness' found expression varies considerably, it embodies a challenge to rigid social conformity. It is at the heart of Ibsen's work, and in the early nineties *Ghosts, Hedda Gabler*, and *A Doll's House* made their dramatic impact on the English stage. In *Ghosts* the stifling bric-à-brac of middle-class social life is not merely repressive; it is the carrier of a malignant disease. In its review of the first English performance the *Daily Telegraph* responded by calling it 'An open drain, a loathsome sore unbandaged, a dirty act done publicly, or a lazar-house with all its doors and windows open.'[44] It is hard to imagine that Kipling would have been much more in sympathy with Ibsen than he was with Wilde. For him society needs its customs and distinctions; discipline and clean living are solutions to the unreal crises of the effete. The paradox is that he can make us feel the same fear of inescapable contamination, of dreadful unfairness. In a figure like Dowse he apprehends the shrinking of the spirit, the atrophying of George Eliot's 'roaring nature', which he almost obstinately refuses to accept.

Although Kipling clearly belongs to no 'set' or group of writers, the presence in his writing of themes and motifs and preoccupations that are to be found among aesthetes and decadents, naturalists and evolutionary pessimists, Fabians and socialists, is more than tangential. Dick Heldar's friend Torpenhow describes his Melancolia for us as a woman who 'has seen the game played out – I don't think she had a good time of it – and now she doesn't care.' As early as 1891 the *Saturday Review* noted that the motivation behind Kipling's game of life 'is not duty, it is more like the feeling with which a man rows out a course in a losing race – not because he ought, but because it is the game.'[45] On this level, as well as in his involvement with the popular forms and fashions – 'slum-fiction', the 'New Woman', writing for children – Kipling is very much part of his period. The despair in Kipling has always been apparent to critics. As David Daiches put it more recently, 'for all his insistence on codes . . . for all his awareness of the ultimate sanctions that keep society from going over the edge . . . there is something very like nihilism at the heart of his work.'[46] To others, both the sanctions and the despair amount to literary cowardice. Boris Ford drew a parallel between Kipling's faith in Empire and the many writers of the nineties – Wilde and Beardsley most dramatically – who found solace in the Catholic Church. This, he argued, was commensurate with a failure in their work to see life steady and whole.[47] Thus, as the initial belief that he was producing an organic and varied world receded, Kipling suffered along with his contemporaries from the long-lasting effects of the literary theory inspired by Matthew Arnold. It is the same view that Richard Le Gallienne expressed in the nineties when he said that 'In decadent literature, the relations, the due proportions are ignored. One might say that literary decadence consists in the euphuistic expression of isolated observations.'[48] Although Kipling's stories are very different indeed from the output of decadent literature they do, at times, lack proportion in Le Gallienne's sense, which has to do with their broad 'moral' as much as formal qualities. The reaction in his work against the 'softness and sweetness of civilisation' also includes an understanding of the isolation and harshness to be encountered within civilisation. His relationship to the culture of the period is complex and frequently self-conscious. In his writing about India there is always a tension between the narrator's role as spectator and the need to offer up an India which mirrors 'ourselves'. The effect of this tension is, sometimes, to make his stories remote not with the factitious 'remoteness' of India, but with a feeling of remoteness that catches the reader off-balance. It is not the absolute emptiness of his world but the feeling that it is off-centre, and that in it the rules of society affect people differently and more drastically. This seems unlikely to be due to any programmatic intention on Kipling's part. We may rather suspect the reverse from, for example, his regret at being unable to build a three-volume novel in the Victorian tradition: 'an East Indiaman worthy to lie alongside *The Cloister and the Hearth*'.[49] The fact that he was an outsider in literary London; that he deliberately wrote for a mass audience while some of his contemporaries at least asserted that they did not; that the India about which he wrote was at once a new subject and one that aroused certain expectations: these are all circumstances which help to explain why the abyss, as J. M. S. Tompkins rightly perceives, opens only on the rim or somewhere in the middle of his tales.

Conclusions

Science and morals are subservient to the reproductive activity; that is why they are so imperative. The rest is what we will, play, art, consolation – in one word religion. If religion is not science or morals, it is the sum of the unfettered impulses of our being. Life has been defined as, even physically and chemically, a tension. All our lives long we are struggling against that tension, but we can only escape from it by escaping from life itself. Religion is the stretching forth of our hands . . . a halfway house on the road to that City which we name mysteriously Death.[1]

So runs the final paragraph of Havelock Ellis's collection of essays, *The New Spirit*, which appeared, to a bad press, in 1890. His treatment of religion is sufficient to account for most of the hostility, but his words are surely as characteristic an expression of the 'New Spirit', the mood of the moment, as he intended them to be. It is indeed *too* characteristic to be very inspiring, with its 'unfettered impulses' on one side, and its 'tension' and 'struggle' on the other. The feeling it expresses is a commonplace of the period that aims no further, lacking the urgency of at least some of the contributions of the time to aesthetic and social questioning. The half-hearted toying with religion-as-metaphor is in reality rather flaccid. In the nineties everyone was chasing the prefix 'New', and the young Kipling was one among others in whom having something new to say sometimes produced knowingness rather than a real desire for knowledge:

> Lalun is a member of the most ancient profession in the world. Lilith was her very-great-grandmama, and that was before the days of Eve, as everyone knows. In the West, people say rude things about Lalun's profession, and write lectures about it, and distribute the lectures to young persons in order that Morality may be preserved. In the East, where the profession is hereditary, descending from mother to daughter, nobody writes lectures or takes any notice; and that is a distinct proof of the inability of the East to manage its own affairs.[2]

This is more uninterested, and therefore uninteresting, than it is disinterested. Even in his best work, Kipling is capable of lapsing into generalities and becoming 'knowing' and superficial as a result. In some of his early stories especially he is prone to begin with a display of sententiousness. In 'The Drums of the Fore and Aft' he clearly understands the condition of the English working classes; but he sketches them at arm's length in a way that compares unfavourably with, for example, the groping sincerity with which Gissing tries to weigh up Richard Mutimer in *Demos*. Although it would be specious to criticise Kipling for not being a novelist, there are certainly times when his intentions are all too clear, and the types he portrays act as little more than mouthpieces. Tracing the acceleration of the decline in literary quality in most fiction from about Kipling's time, Q. D. Leavis remarked that 'In the best-seller as we have known it since the author has poured his own day-dreams, hot and hot, into dramatic form . . . the author himself – or more usually herself – identified with the leading character, and the reader is invited to share in the debauch.'[3] Francis Adams found fault with Kipling's characterisation on just these grounds: 'Instances of this sort of utterly inartistic insertion of little bits of Mr Rudyard Kipling into Mr Rudyard Kipling's "rude figures of a rough-hewn race" are very plentiful, and are certainly not edifying samples of the way he shows his "power over these".[4] Although the charge is a broad one, the point can be readily taken by calling to mind, for example, the Ortheris who declines to ' "go whinin' about my rights to this an' my rights to that, just as if I couldn't look after myself." '

This said, Kipling's prejudices and preferences are no more than a minor element in his work. His motive may have been to justify the Empire, but he was deeply concerned with making sense of India, and did not underestimate his task. In describing popular representations of empire, Ariel Dorfman has used the analogy of the mansions in the American South, where the slaves' quarters only have been demolished. Similarly, he says, 'Each of the Lone Ranger's episodes (and every adventure in every subliterary publication) is an act of omission, a silence, a history book with blank pages.'[5] We can at least conclude that Kipling's omissions are not entirely of this subliterary kind. On the contrary, he went beyond the assortment of stereotypes that made up his readers' conception of India in ways that were potentially disturbing. The controlling spirit in his prose indicates the presence of awkward realities rather than their omission. In bringing India to a new reading public, however, Kipling was, inevitably, concerned to a large extent with the surfaces of this world, and with utilising his skills as 'reporter'. As Raymond Williams has written in connection with George Orwell, 'a restless society very easily accepts this kind of achievement: at one level the report on the curious or the exotic; at another level, when the class or society is nearer the reporter's own, the perceptive critique.'[6] Both this and the noting of Orwell's literary use of 'provocative assertion' can well be applied to Kipling. But the reporter may be, in Williams' suggestive terminology, either an 'exile' or a 'vagrant': and here the resemblance with Kipling ends. Kipling has none of the necessary coldness and detachment that this implies. He is, on the contrary, always the 'insider', if not always by any means a happy or confident one. For this reason his attempts at satire are never very successful: his exposure of his quarry is always compromised by a pre-judged exclusion of the type in question from decent society. The steadily increasing number of studies sympathetic to Kipling have a great deal to confront in the judgement that passes from Henry James to Vernon Lee and Q. D. Leavis, and from them to C. S. Lewis and Boris Ford: that Kipling's fictional world is too narrow, inhabited by types rather than individuals, and marred by didacticism and special pleading. It is against this formidable background that a case must be put for the abiding interest of his work.

If it is accepted that Kipling is often, in every sense, a 'reporter', note must be taken of the circumstances that surround his role as intermediary between British society and India. To the British of Kipling's time India is at once entirely 'foreign', and at the same time a mirroring device in which they expect to see a reflection that is in some way exemplary. It has to be remembered that they were not strongly disposed to take any great interest in India at all. It would scarcely have been possible in these circumstances for Kipling to write with any real detachment, and although he made full use of the journalist as a persona, he never seriously pretended to be doing so. For his British as much as for his Anglo-Indian audience he sees himself much more as the insider than the outsider. Allusions to Rome, the bridge as a metaphor for civilisation, the close association of political with sexual conquest and the accompanying fear of the process spinning out of control, are all part of a stance that the British had already adopted, but which needed a Kipling to bring it to life.

Whatever the relative success of individual stories in using India within such limits, finding an appropriate and fertile relationship between what the British thought and the India that he knew presented Kipling with a problem. The Anglo-Indian novel, as represented by Mrs Steel, presented a fictional world in which 'sahib' and 'native' moved in separate spheres; their conflicting values held up for inspection. The only model of close contact between races on offer was the extreme one of rape, but until it became possible for E. M. Forster to expose its mythic aspect this was not a theme that offered great literary possibilities. It is useful to compare the fictional treatment of the 'native' with the treatment of the English working-class at a slightly earlier period. George Eliot's *Felix Holt, the Radical* and Gissing's *Demos* offer two examples of novels in which the upper class, the gentility and the repositories of cultural and spiritual value, are threatened by a working-class incursion. Different as they are in many respects, these two novels, which by no means radiate optimism about the rising working-class, are nevertheless able to enmesh its representatives in the story. The plots of both turn on an inheritance, and both are to a great extent concerned with distinguishing the true gentleman both from the phoney (Christian and Jermyn in *Felix Holt*, Rodman in *Demos*) and from the novel phenomenon of the non-gentleman (Mutimer and Felix). The kind of weighing up of different sets of values and priorities that this process implies is precisely what the predetermined notions about the sahib-native relationship preclude, and it is the process that gives vitality to both novels, although we are never in much doubt about the conservatism of either author (the admiration bestowed upon Felix is clearly due to the fact that he is in reality more a spiritual than a political reformer). This, then, is one of the problems that faced Kipling in bringing India close to his readers. In a sense he had no choice but to celebrate the fact of British rule, since India as it was then conceived could not be imagined putting out a *challenge* as the English working class might. Its threat, climate apart, reduces itself to mere barbarism, rape and pillage, not a question of conflicting values at all – except at a level of bland abstraction. It is, in fact, disease and isolation which exacerbate the domestic difficulties of the Anglo-Indian community, and make their hold on their ordered lives a precarious matter.

In discovering a subject in the British soldier, it is not too much to say that Kipling discovered at least a partial solution to the problem of fictionalising India. Mulvaney, Learoyd, and Ortheris are regional types, and their identities are very much bound up with being soldiers, but the distance at which they are held by the authorial perspective is much the same as in *Demos*. We are asked not to identify, but to note both their resemblance to ourselves and the crucial restrictions upon it. Chief among these, perhaps, is the innately destructive tendency of working-class man, and his lack of culture. Destructiveness may be useful for the private soldier, but it is always clear that this depends upon his being strictly at the command of his superiors. Unlike Gissing's socialist, Kipling's soldier can respond to natural beauty; but the response is merely sensuous, not 'educated'. The leaven of culture is irremediably absent, and the working class are in a degraded state which society is obliged both to ameliorate and to control. Kipling has only one traditional solution – conscription – to offer. The general state may occasionally be transcended by a working-class woman of special purity and devotion (Gissing's Emma Vine; Kipling's Dinah Shadd and Badalia Herodsfoot), who may bring a momentary grace to her environment, as Dinah's hand falls into Mulvaney's 'like a rose-leaf into a muddy road.'[7]

In the soldier stories the notion of India as a dark, disturbing presence, a fevering agent, can come more fully into play because the working-class soldier is by his nature more susceptible to its influence, while at the same time he is more physically enclosed by his barracks. There is a real involvement here with an 'India', but it takes the stylised form of a series of temptations and difficulties. Mulvaney, the good soldier who accepts his place in society and upholds standards of decency, is still engaged in a struggle against his own animal nature. For less stable individuals with less decent instincts Kipling can supply a grim account of what India may hold in store. The contrast between Mulvaney and Love-o'-Women is partly one of class, for the latter's sense of damnation (and Mulvaney's sense of his damnation) stems from the fact that he was once a gentleman. The depths of suffering are reserved for Holden in 'Without Benefit of Clergy'. He has the devotion and fidelity of a fully civilised man, and his loss is porportionally greater.

The precarious enclosed spaces of all these stories provide a situation in which India can be felt as an active presence, both hostile and alluring. It does not in itself challenge or call into question middle-class values, but it provides a context in which the preoccupations of the middle-class Victorian male can be reflected. Paradoxically, Kipling's stories of 'native life' lose touch with the pressure that India exerts in this way. In direct confrontation with the native world the sahib exhibits an untroubled superiority over people whose lives are either as remote to him as legend or else comically primitive. *Kim* attempts to attribute to the native world a set of values that harmonise with those of the white man, but the sensuous, more rounded India that results is largely the land of Kipling's own legend, a reflection of his own desire for an India that is happily married to England and integral to its way of life.

But although he always allied himself with a particular group, party, and political framework, Kipling did have at times the sharpness of perception of an outsider in his own society. The position in which he found himself as an Anglo-Indian writer in London – well-connected but also somewhat 'provincial'; a writer of unusual talents but slightly dubious credentials, obviously did nothing to blunt this, and led to conflicts in which much of the virulence was on Kipling's side. But it also made him highly sensitive to the changing nature of his society. His partisanship did not prevent him from sensing that it was not just a small, decadent élite, but his period as a whole that had lost faith in the well-ordered society and was coming to look on life as a tense, isolated struggle for existence. The evidence for this is not the frequency with which his characters step away from the paths of simple duty and sexual morality, though it suggested to his readers that something was amiss. It is the way in which the moral is wrenched home, or that the characters seem suddenly to exist in a different, more terrible world. The extent to which this happens at all varies considerably, even among Kipling's best stories. Although there is a feeling of tension in 'The Incarnation of Krishna Mulvaney' and 'The Head of the District', for example, it has not reached the pitch at which bafflement sets in. The project of 'Krishna Mulvaney' is to describe the life and purpose of the 'Tommy', and it is brought firmly back to that point. The project of 'The Head of the District' is to insist on the clear understanding of the basic relationship between sahib and native on which any political change in India must be based. Perhaps 'Love-o'-Women' and 'Without Benefit of Clergy' can equally be said to have such a project, but in their cases the project concerns us no longer. The tension itself has taken over these stories and vitiated any plain-faced 'educative' function. At such moments Kipling's assured style reveals more than it purports to. He can give his robust figures no immunity from the corruption that he fears. Disguised by his vision of Empire the seeds are present, in the early work, of Kipling's preoccupation in the second half of his life with the mysterious knots of suffering and disease.

For all the bias in matters of race and class that he displays, and his tendency to see the archetypal imperialist as an infallible being, Kipling is very much a puritan in this: that those who transgress against society cannot recover, for the stability that society offers only exists, precariously, to the extent to which individuals are prepared to uphold it. It is true that Trejago, in 'Beyond the Pale', returns to everyday society, but he stands in contrast with Dowse the lighthouse keeper who can never recover his self-esteem, Love-o'-Women in his hell, and Holden, who cannot be imagined recovering from the brutal annihilation of his private world in any meaningful sense. Such a view of society makes life a minefield for the individual whatever his advantages, and its grimness is increased when the person who holds it is tempted to the violent conclusion of Dick Heldar: that society in its current state is not worth having. The outburst of *The Light That Failed* is at once revealing of Kipling's particular state of mind, and typical of the period in its retreat into the viewpoint of a small band of like-minded individuals who declare that ordinary society does not fulfil their emotional needs.

In the end it is hard to avoid the feeling that Kipling craved the security which Dick Heldar is certain not to find, and which Kim only possesses in an India of preternatural pastoral innocence. In his short fiction we cannot overlook the extent to which he makes things easy, familiar, and reassuring for the reader, but neither should we ignore the perturbation that affects these stories in varying degrees; the unusual pain with which he propounds the commonplace idea that life is fraught with inevitable tension.

Select Bibliography

Ballhatchet, Kenneth, *Race, Sex and Class under the Raj*, (London: Weidenfield & Nicholson, 1982).
Birkenhead, Earl of, *Rudyard Kipling*, (London: Weidenfeld & Nicholson, 1978).
Carrington, Charles, *Rudyard Kipling: His Life and Work* (Harmondsworth: Penguin Books, 1970; London: Macmillan, 1955).
Cornell, Louis, *Kipling in India* (London: Macmillan, 1966).
Gilbert, Elliott L. (ed.), *Kipling and the Critics* (London: Peter Owen, 1966).
Green, Roger Lancelyn (ed.), *Kipling: The Critical Heritage*, (London: Routledge & Kegan Paul, 1971).
Gross, John (ed.), *Rudyard Kipling: the man, his work, and his world*, (London: Weidenfeld & Nicholson, 1969).
Rutherford, Andrew (ed.), *Kipling's Mind and Art*, (London: Oliver & Boyd, 1964).
Said, Edward, *Orientalism*, (London: Routledge & Kegan Paul, 1978).
Tompkins, J. M. S., *The Art of Rudyard Kipling*, (London: Methuen, 1959).
Williams, Raymond, *Culture and Society*, (Harmondsworth: Penguin Books, 1963).

Appendix

An alphabetical list of stories referred to in the text, with details of original publication and volume in which collected.

NOTES

> *Under the Deodars* and *The Phantom Rickshaw* have frequently been incorporated under the volume title *Wee Willie Winkie*; likewise *The Story of the Gadsbys* and *In Black and White* may often be located in *Soldiers Three*.
>
> C & MG — *Civil and Military Gazette*, Lahore
> Plain Tales — *Plain Tales from the Hills*

.007 (*Scribner's Magazine*, August 1897); *The Day's Work*.
At the End of the Passage (*Lippincott's*, August 1890); *Life's Handicap*.
At Twenty-Two (*Week's News*, Allahabad, 18 February 1888); *In Black and White*.
Below the Mill Dam, *Traffics and Discoveries* (1904).
Beyond the Pale, *Plain Tales*.
Big Drunk Draf', The (*Week's News*, Allahabad, 24 March 1888); *Soldiers Three*.
Black Jack, *Soldiers Three*.
Bridge-Builders, The (*Illustrated London News*, Christmas 1893); *The Day's Work*.
Brugglesmith (*Week's News*, 31 October 1891; *Black and White Magazine*, October 1891; *Harper's Weekly*, 17 October 1891); *Many Inventions*.
Brushwood Boy, The (*Country Magazine*, 1895); *The Day's Work*.
City of Dreadful Night, The (*C & MG*, 20 September 1885); *Life's Handicap*.
Conversion of Aurelian McGoggin, The (*C & MG*, 28 April 1887); *Plain Tales*.
Courting of Dinah Shadd, The (*Macmillan's Magazine*, March 1890; *Living Age*, May 1890); *Life's Handicap*.
Disturber of Traffic, A (*Atlantic Monthly*, September 1891); *Many Inventions*.
Dray Wara Yow Dee (*Week's News*, Allahabad, 28 April 1888); *In Black and White*.
Dream of Duncan Parrenness, The, *Life's Handicap*.
Drums of the Fore and Aft, The, *Wee Willie Winkie*.
False Dawn, *Plain Tales*.
For One Night Only (*Longman's Magazine*, April 1890).
Friendly Brook, *A Diversity of Creatures* (1917).
Gardener, The, *Debits and Credits* (1926).
Gate of the Hundred Sorrows, The (*C & MG*, 26 September 1884); *Plain Tales*.

Georgie Porgie, *Life's Handicap.*
God from the Machine, The (*Week's News*, Allahabad, 7 January 1888); *Soldiers Three.*
Head of the District, The (*Macmillan's Magazine*, January 1890); *Life's Handicap.*
His Chance in Life (*C & MG*, 2 April 1887); *Plain Tales.*
His Private Honour (*Macmillan's Magazine*, October 1891); *Many Inventions.*
How Fear Came, *The Second Jungle Book.*
How the Whale got his Throat, *Just-So Stories.*
In Flood Time (*Week's News*, Allahabad, 11 August 1888); *In Black and White.*
In the Matter of a Private (*Week's News*, Allahabad, 14 April 1888); *Soldiers Three.*
Incarnation of Krishna Mulvaney, The (*Macmillan's Magazine*, December 1889); *Life's Handicap.*
Judgement of Dungara, The (*Week's News*, Allahabad, 28 July 1888); *In Black and White.*
Kaa's Hunting (*McClure's Magazine*, June 1894); *The Jungle Book.*
Kidnapped (*C & MG*, 21 March 1887); *Plain Tales.*
King's Ankus, The (*St Nicholas*, March 1895); *The Second Jungle Book.*
Lamentable Comedy of Willow Wood, The (*Fortnightly Review*, May 1890).
Legs of Sister Ursula, The (*The Idler*, June 1893; *McClure's Magazine*, March 1894).
Letting In the Jungle (*McClure's Magazine*, January 1895); *The Second Jungle Book.*
Lispeth (*C & MG*, 29 November 1886); *Plain Tales.*
'Love-o'-Women', *Many Inventions.*
Madness of Private Ortheris, The, *Plain Tales.*
Man Who Would Be King, The, *The Phantom Rickshaw.*
Mark of the Beast, The (*Pioneer*, Allahabad, 12 & 14 July 1890); *Life's Handicap.*
Mary Postgate, *A Diversity of Creatures* (1917).
Miracle of Purun Bhagat, The, *The Second Jungle Book.*
Miss Youghal's Sais (*C & MG*, 25 April 1887); *Plain Tales.*
Mother Hive, The, *Actions and Reactions* (1909).
Mowgli's Brothers, *The Jungle Book.*
Mutiny of the Mavericks, The, *Life's Handicap.*
My Great and Only (*C & MG*, 11 January 1890); *Abaft the Funnel.*
My Lord the Elephant (*Macmillan's Magazine*, June 1893); *Many Inventions.*
On Greenhow Hill (*Macmillan's Magazine*, September 1890); *Life's Handicap.*
On the City Wall, *In Black and White.*
One View of the Question (*Fortnightly Review*, February 1890); *Many Inventions.*
Only a Subaltern (*Week's News*, Allahabad, 25 August 1888); *Under the Deodars.*
Phantom Rickshaw, The, *Quartette* (1885); *The Phantom Rickshaw.*
Potted Princess, The (*St Nicholas*, January 1893).

Record of Badalia Herodsfoot, The (*Harper's Weekly*, 15 & 22 November, 1890); *Many Inventions*.
Red Dog, *The Second Jungle Book*.
Return of Imray, The, *Life's Handicap*.
Rikki Tikki Tavi, *The Jungle Book*.
Ship that Found Herself, The, (*Idler*, December 1895; *McClure's Magazine*, March 1896); *The Day's Work*.
Spring Running, The (as 'Mowgli Leaves The Jungle', *Cosmopolitan*, October 1895); *The Second Jungle Book*.
Story of Muhammed Din, The, (*C & MG*, 8 September 1886); *Plain Tales*.
Story of the Gadsbys, The, (*Week's News*, Allahabad, 26 May – 7 July 1888).
Strange Ride of Morrowbie Jukes, The, *Quartette* (1885); *The Phantom Rickshaw*.
Taking of Lungtunpen, The (*C & MG*, 11 April 1887); *Plain Tales*.
Through the Fire (*C & MG*, 28 May 1888); *Life's Handicap*.
Tiger, Tiger!, *The Jungle Book*.
To be Filed for Reference, *Plain Tales*.
Tod's Amendment, *Plain Tales*.
Undertakers, The, *The Second Jungle Book*.
Walking Delegate, A (*Century Magazine*, December 1894); *The Day's Work*.
Wayside Comedy, A (*Week's News*, Allahabad, 21 January 1888); *Under the Deodars*.
Wee Willie Winkie (*Week's News*, Allahabad, 28 January 1888); *Wee Willie Winkie*.
White Seal, The (*Nation*, August 1893); *The Jungle Book*.
William the Conqueror (*The Gentlewoman*, December 1895; *Ladies' Home Journal*, January 1896); *The Day's Work*.
With the Main Guard (*Week's News*, Allahabad, 4 August 1888; *Harper's Weekly*, 7 & 14 June 1890); *Soldiers Three*.
Without Benefit of Clergy (*Macmillan's Magazine*, June 1890); *Life's Handicap*.
Wish House, The, *Debits and Credits* (1926).
'Yoked with an Unbeliever' (*C & MG*, 7 December 1886); *Plain Tales*.

Notes and References

1: A BRITISH VIEW OF INDIA

1. By the balladeer G. W. Hunt; performed by 'The Great Macdermott'.
2. (a) Thomas Carlyle, 'Occasional Discourse on the Nigger Question', *Critical and Miscellaneous Essays VI* (London: Chapman and Hall, 1869) pp. 173–4 & p. 203; (b) John Ruskin, *Collected Works of John Ruskin* (London: George Allen, 1905), vol. XVI pp. 261–2.
3. A. P. Thornton, *Doctrines of Imperialism* (New York: John Wiley & Sons, 1965) pp. 23 & 26; Benjamin Disraeli, *Tancred* (London: Longman, Green & Co., 1882) p. 141.
4. E. J. Hobsbawm, *Industry and Empire* (Harmondsworth: Penguin Books, 1969) p. 239.
5. Holbrook Jackson, *The Eighteen Nineties* (London: Grant Richards, 1913) p. 237.
6. Edward Said, *Orientalism* (London: Routledge & Kegan Paul, 1978) p. 206.
7. See Plate 2.
8. John Murray, *A Handbook for Travellers in India, Burma and Ceylon* (London, 1904)
9. James Grant, *Cassell's Illustrated History of India*, vol. 2 (London: Cassell, Petter & Galpin, 1877) p. 269.
10. Grant, *Cassell's Illustrated History*, p. 261.
11. J. Talboys Wheeler, *A College History of India* (London: Macmillan, 1888).
12. R. W. Frazer, *British India* (London: T. Fisher Unwin, 1898) p. 276.
13. Frazer, *British India*, p. 321.
14. Flora Annie Steel, *On the Face of the Waters: a novel of the Indian Mutiny* (London: William Heinemann, 1896).
15. Grant, *Cassell's Illustrated History*, p. 268.
16. 'The Taking of Lungtunpen'.
17. Emily Eden, *Up the Country*, 2 (London: Richard Bentley, 1866) p. 133.
18. Frank Richards, *Old Soldier Sahib* (London: Faber, 1936) p. 75.
19. T. W. Holderness, *Peoples and Problems of India* (London: Home University Press, 1913) p. 69.
20. Holderness, *People and Problems of India*, pp. 71 and 93.
21. 'Mr Kipling's Stories' in R. L. Green (ed.), *Kipling: The Critical Heritage* (London: Routledge & Kegan Paul, 1971) p. 154.
22. 'Egypt of the Magicians' (1913), from *Letters of Travel*.
23. *The Day's Work* (1898).
24. F. H. Skrine, *The Life of Sir William Wilson Hunter* (London: Longman, Green & Co., 1902) p. 442.
25. Kipling wrote some hostile articles on these topics early in his career.
26. John Lockwood Kipling, *Beast and Man in India* (London: Macmillan, 1892) p. 21.

27. A useful account of J. L. Kipling's work is given by Mahrukh Tarapor, 'John Lockwood Kipling and Art Education in India', *Victorian Studies*, 24, 1980, No. 1.
28. Grant, *Cassell's Illustrated History*, p. 543.
29. J. L. Kipling, *Beast and Man in India*, p. 157; Holderness, *People and Problems of India*, p. 248.
30. Eden, *Up the Country*, p. 161.
31. Ibid, p. 229.
32. Richard Le Gallienne, *Rudyard Kipling: An Appreciation* (London: John Lane, 1900) p. 57.
33. 'Yoked with an Unbeliever'.
34. J. L. Kipling, *Beast and Man in India*, p. 31.
35. Eden, *Up the Country*, pp. 138–9.
36. Holderness, *People and Problems of India*, p. 92.
37. Coventry Patmore, *The Angel in the House*, Bk 1, Canto IV, Preludes 2 (London: Macmillan, 1863) pp. 52–3.
38. A. F. Sandys shared Rossetti's studio in Cheyne Walk for a time. His striking 'Medea' was turned down by the Royal Academy in 1868, to the disgust of Rossetti and Swinburne, who protested publicly.
39. (Maud Diver) See Frances Mannsaker, 'Anglo-Indian Racial Attitudes', *Victorian Studies*, 24, 1980, No. 1, pp. 38–9. The Kipling story is 'His Chance in Life'.
40. Meredith Townsend, 'Will England Retain India?', *Contemporary Review*, 53 (June 1888) p. 803.
41. Charles Carrington, *Rudyard Kipling – His Life and Work* (Harmondsworth: Penguin Books, 1970) p. 103.
42. *The Saturday Review*, LXXIV, 20 August 1892, p. 226; Grant, *Cassell's Illustrated History*, p. 237.
43. Holderness, *People and Problems of India*, p. 57.
44. Eden, *Up the Country*, pp. 231–2.
45. 'Rudyard Kipling' in Green, *Kipling: The Critical Heritage*, p. 349.
46. Holderness, *People and Problems of India*, p. 16.
47. Thomas Huxley, *Evolution and Ethics* (London: Macmillan, 1895) pp. 16–17.
48. *Something of Myself* (3).
49. Eden, *Up the Country*, pp. 110–11.
50. 'The Judgement of Dungara'.
51. Dennis Kincaid, *British Social Life in India, 1608–1937* (London: Routledge & Kegan Paul, 1938) p. 200.
52. 'Tod's Amendment'; *Kim* (13).
53. Green, *Kipling: The Critical Heritage*, p. 153.
54. R. F. Betts, 'Allusions to Rome in British Imperialist Thought', *Victorian Studies*, 15, December 1971, p. 155; James Joyce, *Ulysses* (London: Bodley Head, 1960) p. 132.
55. *Punch*, 3 May 1890, p. 206.
56. Ruskin, *Collected Works*, Vol xx, p. 42.
57. Wheeler, *A College History of India*, p. 207; Kipling, *From Sea to Sea* (VII).
58. 'A Matter of Vision: Rudyard Kipling and Rider Haggard', in John

Notes and References 141

Gross (ed.) *Rudyard Kipling: The Man, his Work, and his World* (London: Weidenfeld & Nicholson, 1969) p. 128.

2: EARLY STAGES

1. Louis Cornell, *Kipling in India* (London: Macmillan, 1966) p. 91.
2. Suzanne Howe (Nobbe), *Novels of Empire* (New York: Columbia University Press, 1949) p. 37.
3. David Galloway (ed.), *Selected Writings of Edgar Allan Poe* (Harmondsworth: Penguin Books, 1967) p. 532. Recalls the story's appearance in a medical journal.
4. Cornell, *Kipling in India*, pp. 156–9.
5. Philip Mason, *The Glass, the Shadow, and the Fire* (London: Jonathan Cape, 1975) p. 51.
6. 'The True Function and Value of Criticism' in Green, *Kipling: The Critical Heritage*, p. 104.
7. 'For I consort with long-haired things/In velvet collar-rolls . . . ' From 'In Partibus'.
8. Green, *Kipling: The Critical Heritage*, p. 105.
9. *The Saturday Review*, 20 October 1888, p. 470.
10. 'The Tales of Rudyard Kipling', *Edinburgh Review*, CLXXIV (July–October 1891) p. 133.
11. From (a) 'The English Flag' and (b) 'The Drums of the Fore and Aft'.
12. Suzanne Howe, *Novels of Empire*, p. 78.
13. Cornell, *Kipling in India*, p. 123.
14. Green, *Kipling: The Critical Heritage*, pp. 47–9.
15. Ibid, pp. 233 and 307.
16. Martin Fido, *Rudyard Kipling* (London: Hamlyn, 1974) p. 70.
17. J. M. S. Tompkins, 'Kipling and the Shambles', *Kipling Journal*, December 1965, p. 31.
18. *Something of Myself* (4).
19. Raymond Williams, *Culture and Society* (Harmondsworth: Penguin Books, 1963) p. 119.
20. Edward Said, *Orientalism*, p. 206.
21. Jonah Raskin, *The Mythology of Imperialism* (New York: Random House, 1971) p. 65.

3: SOLDIERS IN INDIA

1. Charles Carrington, *Rudyard Kipling – His Life and Work* (Harmondsworth: Penguin Books, 1970) p. 184.
2. 'Ship me somewheres East of Suez,/Where the best is like the worst,/Where there aren't no Ten Commandments,/An' a man can raise a thirst.' – from 'Mandalay'.
3. Green, *Kipling: The Critical Heritage*, p. 41.
4. In Rudyard Kipling, *The Complete Barrack-Room Ballads* (London: Methuen, 1973) p. 5.

5. 'The Incarnation of Krishna Mulvaney'.
6. 'The God from the Machine'.
7. 'The Courting of Dinah Shadd'.
8. 'Burra Murra Boko by Kippierd Herring' (by R. C. Lehmann), *Punch*, 11 October 1890, p. 173.
9. J. M. S. Tompkins regards it as an unnecessary intrusion. *The Art of Rudyard Kipling*, p. 248.
10. Sir John Seeley was an historian and a proponent of a federated Empire under British leadership. Joseph Chamberlain and Cecil Rhodes need no introduction.
11. Plate 8.
12. Kenneth Ballhatchet, *Race, Sex and Class under the Raj* (London: Weidenfeld and Nicholson, 1978) p. 182.
13. Green, *Kipling: The Critical Heritage*, p. 9.
14. J. H. Fenwick, 'Soldiers Three' in Andrew Rutherford (ed.), *Kipling's Mind and Art* (London: Oliver & Boyd, 1964).
15. Lord Birkenhead, *Rudyard Kipling* (London: Weidenfeld & Nicholson, 1978) p. 70.
16. Buchanan attacked Kipling's *Stalky & Co.* in 'The Voice of the Hooligan' (Green, p. 233), and Rossetti in 'The Fleshly School of Poetry', *Contemporary Review*, October 1871. The quotation here is from J. A. Spender, *The New Fiction* (London: Westminster Gazette Press, 1895) pp. 120–1.
17. 'Kipling' in Elliott L. Gilbert (ed.), *Kipling and the Critics* (London: Peter Owen, 1966) p. 95.
18. James in fact regretted his optimistic judgement. Green, *Kipling: The Critical Heritage*, p. 69.
19. Adrian Poole, *Gissing in Context* (London: Macmillan, 1975) p. 23.
20. 'The Courting of Dinah Shadd'.
21. Sir James Fitzjames Stephen, Letter to *The Times*, 4 January 1878.

4: ILLUSTRATING THE NATIVE FEATURE

1. Green, *Kipling: The Critical Heritage*, p. 153.
2. Richard Le Gallienne, *Rudyard Kipling*, p. 73.
3. 'What is Kim?' in D. W. Jefferson (ed.) *The Morality of Art: Essays in Honour of G. Wilson Knight* (London: Routledge & Kegan Paul, 1969) p. 213.
4. An account of the unpublished draft of *Kim* is given by Margaret Peller Feeley, 'The *Kim* that nobody reads', *Studies in the Novel*, Fall 1981, p. 266.
5. The tradition of espionage in India is described by Michael Edwardes, *Playing the Great Game* (London: Hamish Hamilton, 1975).
6. *Something of Myself* (5).
7. Ibid. (8).
8. Lockwood Kipling's photographed clay figures illustrated *Kim* for its serialisation in *Strand Magazine* (1900).
9. 'The Kipling that nobody read' in Rutherford (ed.) *Kipling's Mind and Art*.

Notes and References   143

10. 'The Finest Story about India – in English' in John Gross (ed.), *Kipling: The man, his work, and his world*, p. 32.
11. James Elliott, *India* (London: Batsford, 1977) p. 127.
12. 'The Kipling that nobody read', *op cit*.
13. Angus Wilson, *The Strange Ride of Rudyard Kipling* (London: Martin, Secker, and Warburg, 1977) p. 127.
14. *Something of Myself* (5).
15. See Carrington, *Rudyard Kipling* (footnote) p. 260.
16. 'Mowgli's Brothers'.
17. Ibid.
18. Ibid.
19. 'Letting In the Jungle'.
20. Ibid.
21. Gillian Beer, *Darwin's Plots: Evolutionary Narrative in Darwin, George Eliot, and Nineteenth Century Fiction* (London: Routledge & Kegan Paul, 1983) p. 24.
22. Carrington, *Rudyard Kipling*, pp. 190–1. The incident was used in *The Light That Failed*.
23. J. A. V. Chapple, *Documentary and Imaginative Literature, 1880–1920* (London: Blandford Press, 1970) p. 185.
24. Elliott L. Gilbert, *The Good Kipling* (Manchester University Press, 1972) p. 43.
25. *The Civil and Military Gazette*, 14 November 1885.
26. *The Athenaeum*, No. 3281, 13 September 1890.
27. Lionel Johnson, *Academy*, 17 October 1891, pp. 327–8.
28. Green, *Kipling: The Critical Heritage*, p. 108.
29. The story first appeared in *The Gentlewoman* for December 1895.

5: KIPLING AND THE EIGHTEEN-NINETIES

1. Adrian Poole, *Gissing in Context* (London: Macmillan, 1975).
2. *The Whirlpool* (1897), (Brighton: Harvester Press, 1972) p. 449.
3. *London and the Life of Literature in Late Victorian England: The Diary of George Gissing, Novelist* (Edited by Pierre Coustillas) (Brighton: Harvester Press, 1978) p. 11.
4. Green, *Kipling: The Critical Heritage*, pp. 64–6.
5. *Something of Myself* (4).
6. See Ann Murtagh, 'The *New Review*: A Glimpse at the Nineties', *Victorian Periodicals Review*, xiv, Spring 1981, No. 1, pp. 11–12.
7. *Something of Myself* (4).
8. Lord Birkenhead, *Rudyard Kipling*, p. 112.
9. 'For One Night Only'.
10. *The World*, 2 April 1890.
11. Carrington, *Rudyard Kipling*, pp. 185 and 244.
12. The story in *The Idler* was entitled 'The Legs of Sister Ursula'. See Appendix.
13. Mrs Oliphant, *The Victorian Age of English Literature*, 2 (London: Percival & Co., 1892) p. 231; Oscar Wilde, *Complete Works* (London: Collins, 1967) p. 1203.

14. Green, *Kipling: The Critical Heritage*, p. 124.
15. *The New Fiction*, p. 41.
16. Mrs Oliphant, *The Victorian Age*, p. 231.
17. F. Marion Crawford, *Mr Isaacs: A Tale of Modern India* (London: Macmillan, 1889) pp. 51–2.
18. Flora Annie Steel, *On the Face of the Waters*, p. 418.
19. Havelock Ellis (ed.), *The Best Plays of John Ford* (London: T. Fisher Unwin, 1888) p. 246.
20. Ibid, p. 344.
21. Ibid, (Introduction) p. xvii.
22. Green, *Kipling: The Critical Heritage*, p. 69.
23. Carrington, *Rudyard Kipling*, p. 213.
24. 'My Great and Only'.
25. Georg Lukacs, *Studies in European Realism* (London: Merlin Press, 1970) pp. 89–90.
26. 'Badalia Herodsfoot' appeared in *Harper's Weekly* for November 1890; Morrison's 'A Street' in *Macmillan's Magazine* for October 1891.
27. 'Thomas Hardy', *Westminster Review*, CXIX, 1883, p. 3.
28. *The Return of the Native* (London: Macmillan, 1968) pp. 75–6.
29. *The Saturday Review*, LXXI, 4 April 1891, p. 418; Ernest Newman, 'Mr Kipling's Stories', *University Magazine*, 1 December 1893.
30. 'Kipling's Entire' from *Around the Theatres*.
31. Green, *Kipling: The Critical Heritage*, pp. 142 and 89; *Review of Reviews*, October 1890, p. 341; *The Athenaeum*, No. 3271, 5 July 1890.
32. 'Kipling's World' in Elliott L. Gilbert (ed.), *Kipling and the Critics*, p. 103.
33. Cf. George Orwell, 'Rudyard Kipling' in Rutherford (ed.), *Kipling's Mind and Art* (London: Oliver & Boyd, 1964), and Jack Dunman, 'Kipling and the Marxists', *Marxism Today*, August 1965.
34. 'One View of the Question'.
35. E. J. Hobsbawm, *Industry and Empire* (Harmondsworth: Penguin Books, 1969) p. 186.
36. Green, *Kipling: The Critical Heritage*, p. 306.
37. J. M. S. Tompkins, *The Art of Rudyard Kipling*, p. 190.
38. Poole, *Gissing in Context*, pp. 48–9.
39. *Vignettes* (London: John Lane, 1896) p. 55.
40. *Esther Waters* (1893) (London: J. M. Dent & Sons, 1977) pp. 165–6.
41. Poole, op. cit., p. 48.
42. George Eliot, *Middlemarch* (Harmondsworth: Penguin Books, 1965) II.20, p. 226.
43. Poole, op. cit., p. 47.
44. Holbrook Jackson, *The Eighteen Nineties*, p. 252.
45. *Saturday Review*, LXXII, 12 September 1892, p. 304.
46. David Daiches, *Some Late Victorian Attitudes* (London: André Deutsch, 1969) p. 26.
47. 'A Case for Kipling?' in Elliott L. Gilbert, *Kipling and the Critics*.
48. Cf. John Goode, 'The Decadent Writer as Producer' in Ian Fletcher (ed.), *Decadence and the 1890s* (London: Edward Arnold, 1979) p. 112.
49. *Something of Myself* (8).

CONCLUSIONS

1. Havelock Ellis, *The New Spirit* (New York: Boni & Liveright, 1921) p. 292.
2. 'On the City Wall'.
3. Q. D. Leavis, *Fiction and the Reading Public* (1932); (Harmondsworth: Penguin Books, 1971) p. 188.
4. Green, *Kipling: The Critical Heritage*, p. 145.
5. *The Empire's Old Clothes* (New York: Pantheon Books/Random House, 1983) p. 63.
6. *Culture and Society*, p. 280.
7. 'The Courting of Dinah Shadd'.

Index

Adams, Francis, 12, 27, 80, 129
Aesthetes, 28, 39, 106, 126
Aesthetic 38–9, 111
Aestheticism, 124
Allen, Grant, 19
Anglo-Indians, 5, 9, 11, 23–8
Athenaeum, The, 101, 119
Auckland, Lord, 10

Babu(s), 13, 41, 86
Balestier, Wolcott, 21
Ballhatchet, Kenneth, 135
Barrack-Room Ballads, The, 50, 60, 103, 117
Beer, Gillian, 96
Beerbohm, Max, 65, 119
Besant, Walter, 105, 117, 124
Birkenhead, Earl of, 135
Blackwood's Magazine, 34
Booth, Charles, 117
Boyce, Lord James, 27
Brahman (Brahmin), 11, 22
Brooke, Charles (Rajah), 77
Buchanan, Robert, 46, 72
Buddhism, 13, 87–8
Burne-Jones, Edward, 31
Burton, Richard, 12
Butler, Josephine, 70
Butterfly, The, 27

Canning, Lord George, 8, 10
Captains Courageous, 90
Carlyle, Thomas, 3
Carrington, Charles, 60, 135
Chamberlain, Joseph, 27, 65
Chambers, Charles Haddon, 71
Chapple, J. A. V., 99
Chaudhuri, Nirad C., 87
Civil and Military Gazette, The, 31, 34, 100
Conrad, Joseph, 53
Contemporary Review, The, 21, 106
Cornell, Louis, 32, 35, 44, 135
Crackanthorpe, Hubert, 123

Crawford, F. Marion, 47, 109–10
Curzon, Lord George Nathaniel, 11–12

Daiches, David, 126
Daily Telegraph, The, 126
Dalhousie, Lord, 8
Darwin, Charles, 38, 96
Darwinism, (Social), 7, 23
Decadent, 38–9, 115, 126–7
Departmental Ditties, 34
Dickens, Charles, 75, 108
Dilke, Charles, 4
Disraeli, Benjamin, 4, 38
Dobrée, Bonamy, 23
Dorfman, Ariel, 129
Dowson, Ernest, 115
Dufferin, Lord, 26
Du Maurier, George, 19
Dyer, Alfred, 27

East India Company, 6
Eden, Emily, 10, 15, 18, 22, 24
Edinburgh Review, The, 40
Eliot, George, 38, 96, 125, 131
Ellis, Havelock, 112, 118, 128
English Illustrated Magazine, The, 34, 106
Eurasian, 20–1, 32, 34, 46, 65, 82

Fenwick, J. H., 68
Fido, Martin, 47
Flaubert, Gustave, 50, 53
Ford, Boris, 126, 130
Ford, John, 112
Forster, E. M., iv, 6, 24, 51, 131
Fortnightly Review, The, 105, 106
From Sea to Sea, 47, 49
Frazer, R. W., 8

Garrard, Violet, 31, 47
Gaskell, Mrs, 38
Gilbert, Elliott L., 99, 135

Index

Gissing, George, 38, 100, 103–4, 107, 117, 129, 131
Gladstone, William Ewart, 2, 4
Gosse, Edmund, 101, 105–7
Gordon, General, 2, 29, 60
Grant, James, 6, 7, 14, 21
Green, Roger Lancelyn, 135
Gross, John, 135
Grove, Archibald, 105

Haggard, Rider, 21, 26, 97, 105, 108
Hardy, Thomas, 30, 38, 71, 96, 99, 103, 105, 108, 119
Harper's Weekly, 106
Harris, Frank, 105
Harrison, Fraser, 15
Hawthorne, Julian, 119
Henley, William Ernest, 105–6
Hill, Professor and Mrs (Edmonia), 91, 105
Holderness, T. W., 7, 11, 18, 83
Howe, Suzanne, 33, 42
Hunter, Sir William Wilson, 13
Huxley, Thomas, 23

Ibsen, Henrik, 54, 71, 116, 126
ICS (Indian Civil Service), 2
Idler, The, 106–7
In Black and White, 55, 100–1
Indian Mutiny, 2, 6–10, 52, 74
Islam, 12

Jackson, Holbrook, 4
James, Henry, 65, 75, 98, 104–6, 112, 130
Jarrell, Randall, 35
Jerome, Jerome K., 107
Jingoism, 2
Johnson, Lionel, 58, 101, 119
Joyce, James, 28
Jungle Books, The, 10, 90–7, 107
Just-So Stories, The, 90, 96

Kafir, 77
Kettle, Arnold, 81
Kim, ix, 10, 11, 13, 17, 21, 26, 31–32, 55, 76, 80–91, 95–6, 133
Kingsley, Mary, 50

Kipling, John Lockwood, 13, 17, 86, 88, 121
Kipling, J. L. and Alice (parents), 21, 31
Kipling, Rudyard, greatest exponent of popular attitude to India, ix; popularity, 1; treatment of sex, 16–17; contribution to Anglo-Indian tradition, 24; involvement with Simla life, 26; vision of Empire, 29–30; also 40, 65; family background, 31–2; journalism, 33–4, also 47–9, 80; literary methods, 85; arrival and reception in London, 104–5, also 124; literary reception (general), 105–8
Kitchener, Lord, 4

Lal Bazaars, 20, 67
Lamarck, Jean-Baptiste, 96
Lang, Andrew, 45, 47, 67, 105
Lawrence, Sir John, 7
Leavis, Q. D., 129–30
Lecky, W., 14
Lee, Vernon, x, 130
Le Gallienne, Richard, 16, 80, 127
Letters of Marque, 23, 47, 97
Lewis, C. S., 120, 130
Life's Handicap, 46, 83, 100–1, 108
Light That Failed, The, 50, 56, 70, 90, 94, 105, 108, 113–5, 119, 134
Lippincott's Monthly Magazine, 106, 114
Lock Hospitals, 20
Longman's Magazine, 106
Loti, Pierre, 40
Lukacs, Georg, 116
Lyall, Sir Alfred, 22

Macaulay, Lord, 2, 7
Macmillan's Magazine, 106
Many Inventions, 125
Mason, Philip, 37
Maupassant, Guy de, 36
Moore, George, 39, 103, 108, 123
Morris, Mowbray, 105
Morris, William, 28, 38

Index

Morrison, Arthur, 116
Mother Maturin, 21
Murray, John, 6

Nation, The, 106
Naulakha, The, 21, 48, 97
New Review, The, 105
Newman, Ernest, 119

Oliphant, Mrs, 107–8, 119
Orientalism, v, 5, 94
Orwell, George, 130
Pall Mall Gazette, The, 106
Passage to India, A, 6, 24, 51
Patmore, Coventry, 19
Pearsall, Ronald, 15
Pioneer, The, 34
Pinero, Arthur Wing, 16, 71
Plain Tales from the Hills, 31, 34, 45, 50, 54
Poe, Edgar Alan, 33
Poems
  Ballad of the *Bolivar*, The, 106
  Buddha at Kamakura, The, 88
  Comforters, The, x
  English Flag, The, 4, 28, 79
  Female of the Species, 20
  Fuzzy-Wuzzy, 9
  In Partibus, 56
  Mandalay, 141
  Mary Gloster, The, 16
  McAndrew's Hymn, 120
  One Viceroy Resigns, 27
  Pagett, M.P., 28
  Paul Vaugel, 32
  Recessional, 104, 122
  Song of the Banjo, The, 105
  Sons of Martha, The, 121
  What the People Said, 8
  Widow at Windsor, The, 63
Poole, Adrian, 75, 103
Pre-Raphaelite, x, 20, 31
Puck of Pook's Hill, 78–9, 90
Punch, 13, 18, 28–9, 62, 117

Quarterly Review, The, 40

Raskin, Jonah, 54
Rewards and Fairies, 90

Rhodes, Cecil, 4, 29, 65
Richards, Frank, 10
Roberts, Lord, 60
Robinson, E. Kay, 34
Rossetti, D. G., 20, 72
Ruskin, John, 3, 28, 114
Rutherford, Andrew, 135

Said, Edward, ix, 5, 53, 135
Saintsbury, George, 105
Sandison, Alan, 30
Sandys, A. F., 20
Saturday Review, The, 119, 126
Savoy Magazine, The, 106
Scots Observer, The, 105–6
Scott, Paul, ix
Seeley, Sir John, 65
Shakespeare, William, 61, 108
Shaw, George Bernard, 28, 103
Singh, Runjit, 18
Soldiers Three, 31, 56, 61
Something of Myself, 32, 40, 43, 78, 85, 124
Spectator, The, 60
Spender, J. A., 107
St James Gazette, The, 106
St Nicholas Magazine, 106
Stalky & Co, 46, 90
Steel, Flora Annie, 9, 18, 26, 47, 111, 131
Stephen, Sir James, 78
Stevenson, Robert Louis, 53, 104
Stoicism, x
Stories
  .007, 120
  At the End of the Passage, 38–9, 44–5
  At Twenty-Two, 116
  Below the Mill Dam, 120
  Beyond the Pale, 16, 35, 37, 49–50, 52, 97, 100, 134
  Big Drunk Draf', The, 74
  Black Jack, 74
  Bridge-Builders, The, 121–3
  Brushwood Boy, The, 58–60
  Conversion of Aurelian McGoggin, The, 35, 80
  Courting of Dinah Shadd, The, 35, 46, 66, 142, 145

Index

Stories – *continued*
Disturber of Traffic, The, 124–5
Dray Wara Yow Dee, 101
Dream of Duncan Parrenness, The, 33
Drums of the Fore and Aft, 129
False Dawn, 26, 46
For One Night Only, 143
Friendly Brook, 90
Gate of the Hundred Sorrows, The, 32–3
Georgie Porgie, 16, 58–9, 73
God from the Machine, The, 142
Head of the District, The, 40–3, 53, 133
His Chance in Life, 82, 140
His Private Honour, 12, 64–5, 82
How Fear Came, 93–6
In The Matter of a Private, 74
Incarnation of Krishna Mulvaney, The, 67–8, 89, 133, 142
Judgement of Dungara, The, 140
Kaa's Hunting, 93
Kidnapped, 34, 46–7
King's Ankus, The, 89, 94
Lamentable Comedy of Willow Wood, The, 124
Legs of Sister Ursula, The, 143
Letting in the Jungle 94–6, 143
Lispeth, 17
Love-o'-Women, 17, 67–74, 90, 112, 133
Madness of Private Ortheris, The, 62–4
Man Who Was, The, 53
Man Who Would Be King, The, 32, 76–9
Mark of the Beast, The, 97
Mary Postgate, 50
Miracle of Purun Bhagat, The, 91
Miss Youghal's Sais, 83
Mother Hive, The, 120
Mowgli's Brothers, 143
Mutiny of the Mavericks, The, 74
My Great and Only, 144
On Greenhow Hill, 46, 50–4, 70, 90
On the City Wall, 145
One View of the Question, 105, 144
Only a Subaltern, 35, 58
Phantom Rickshaw, The, 37
Potted Princess, The, 106
Record of Badalia Herodsfoot, The, 116–19
Red Dog, 94–6
Return of Imray, The, 15
Rikki Tikki Tavi, 91
Ship That Found Herself, The, 120
Spring Running, The, 92
Story of Muhammed Din, The, 36, 83
Story of the Gadsbys, The, 37
Strange Ride of Morrowbie Jukes, The, 33
Taking of Lungtunpen, The, 9
Tiger, Tiger!, 94
To be Filed for Reference, 54, 77
Tod's Amendment, 140
Undertakers, The, 9, 91
Walking Delegate, A, 120
Wayside Comedy, A, 26, 34–6, 40
Wee Willie Winkie, 14
William the Conqueror, 12, 102
Wish House, The, 90
With the Main Guard, 75
Without Benefit of Clergy, 16, 46, 97–100, 110, 132–3
Yoked with an Unbeliever, 140
Strachey, Lytton, 2
Swift, Jonathan, 93

Taylor, Philip Meadows, 110
Thackeray, W. M., 38, 110, 119
Theebaw, King of Burma, 29
Thomson, James, 122
Times, The, 107
Tolstoy, Leo, 99
Tompkins, J. M. S., x, 49, 122, 127, 135
Trilling, Lionel, 73
Twain, Mark (S. L. Clemens), 105

University Review, The, 119

Victoria, Queen, 2, 4, 11, 63
Vizetelly, Henry, 112

Wells, H. G., 28, 46, 103, 121
Wheeler, J. Talboys, 7, 29
Wheeler, Stephen, 34, 105
White, Gilbert, 36
Wilde, Oscar, 38–40, 50, 107, 116, 126

Williams, Raymond, 52–3, 130, 135
Wilson, Angus, 89
Wilson, Edmund, 87–8
Winchester, Mary, 5
Wolseley, Sir Garnet, 60
World, The, 106

Yellow-Book, The, 89, 106

Zola, Emile, 60, 116